# Cats
## and
# Dogs

P.S. MUELLER

**JONES BOOKS** • MADISON WISCONSIN USA

**Jones Books**

309 North Hillside Terrace

Madison, Wisconsin 53705-3328

**www.jonesbooks.com**

Designed by Patrick JB Flynn

Pjbf Design, Madison, Wisconsin

First edition, first printing.

Library of Congress Cataloging-in-Publication Data

Mueller, P. S.

Cats and dogs/dogs and cats / P.S. Mueller.

p. cm.

ISBN 0-9763539-7-0

1. Cats–Caricatures and cartoons. 2. Dogs–Caricatures and cartoons.

3. American wit and humor, Pictorial.

I. Title. II. Title: Cats and dogs. III. Title: Dogs and cats.

NC1429.M87A4 2006

741.5'6973–dc22

2006024618

[PRINTED IN THE UNITED STATES OF AMERICA]

***Thanks*** to: Bob Mankoff at *The New Yorker*, Cameron Woo at *Bark*, Sid Evans and Jean
McKenna at *Field and Stream*, Norman Hotz at *Reader's Digest*, Sam Gross at large upon
the world, David Jones and everyone at the *Chicago Reader*, Ray and Sue and the whole
bunch at *Funny Times*, Joan Strasbaugh at Jones Books, and lastly, Patrick JB Flynn,
who slapped this puppy together.

*Dedicated to my brother*
*Dave*

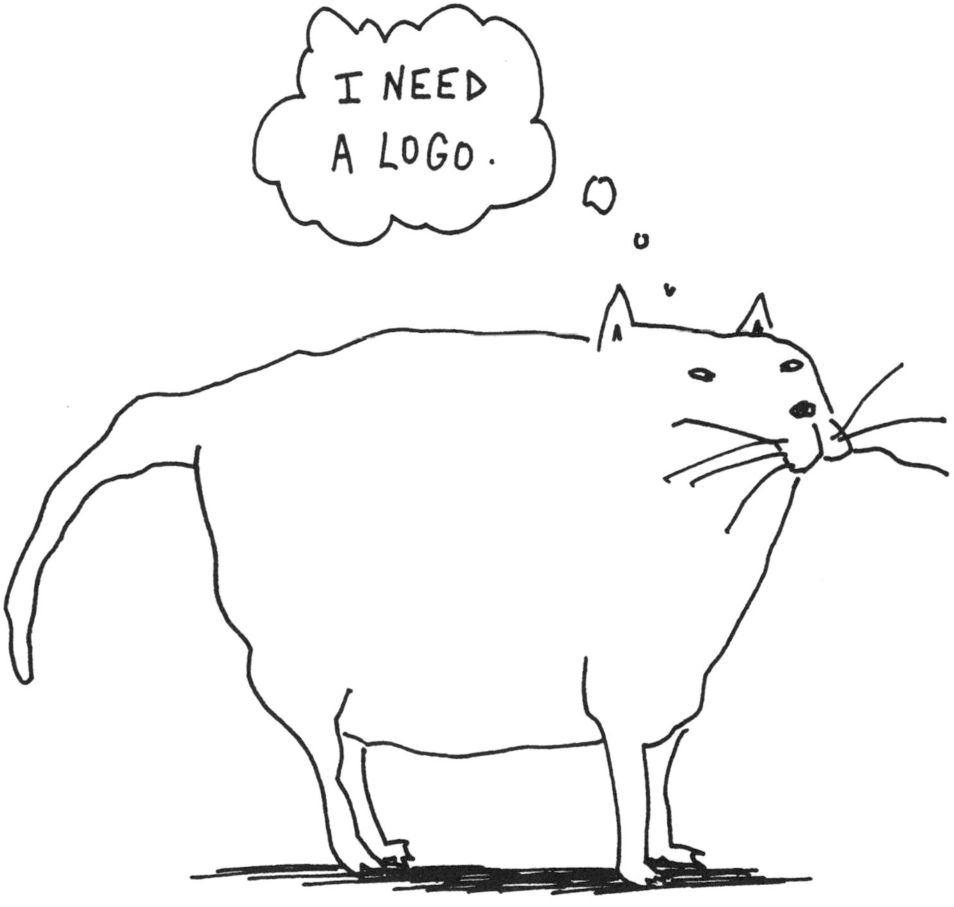
I NEED A LOGO.

BAD INTEL

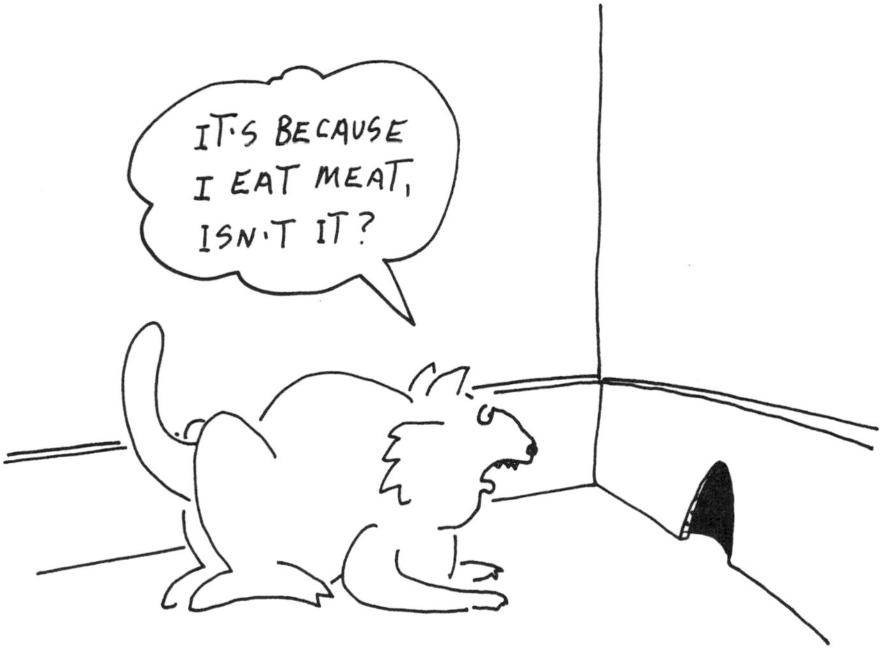
IT'S BECAUSE I EAT MEAT, ISN'T IT?

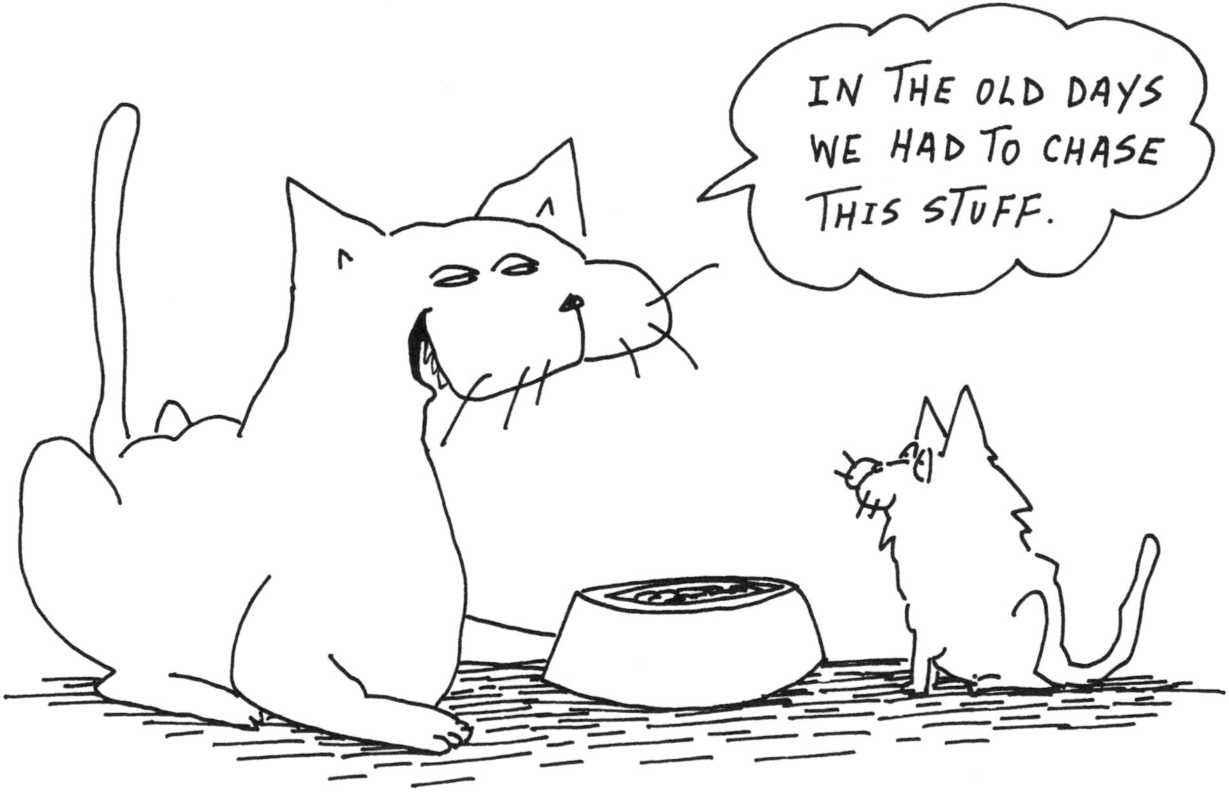
IN THE OLD DAYS WE HAD TO CHASE THIS STUFF.

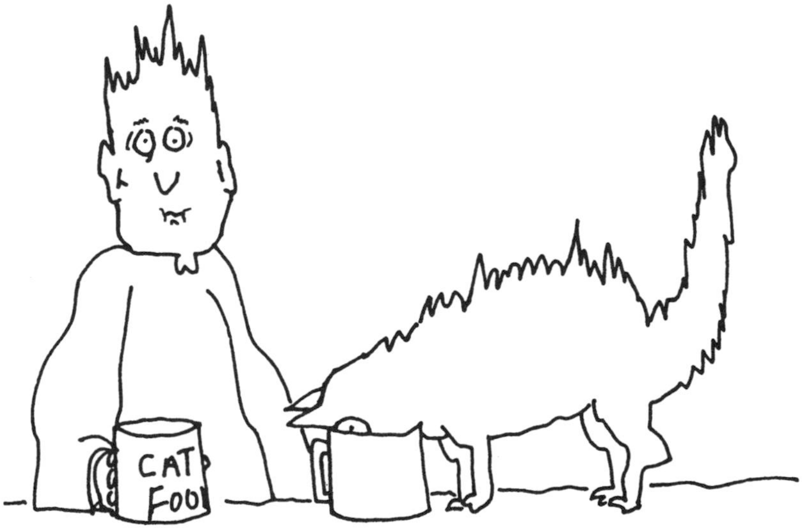
CAT
FOOD

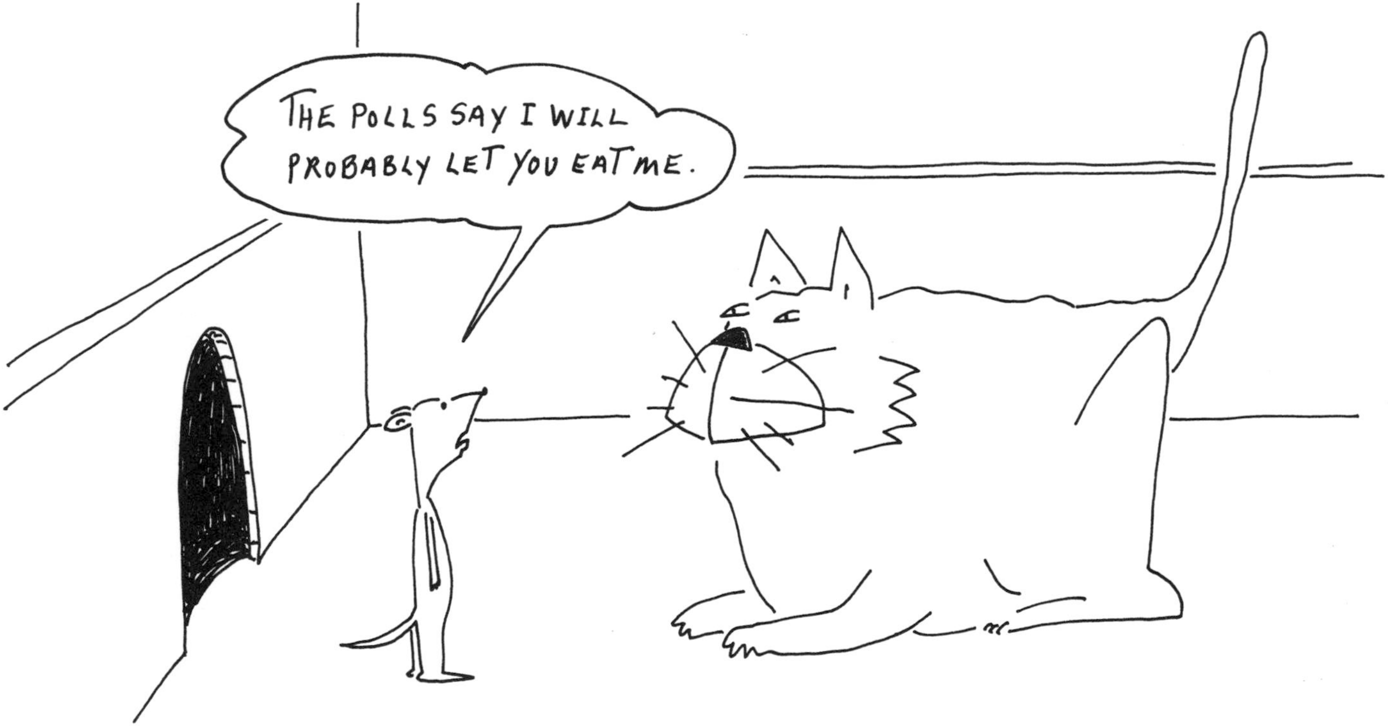
THE POLLS SAY I WILL PROBABLY LET YOU EAT ME.

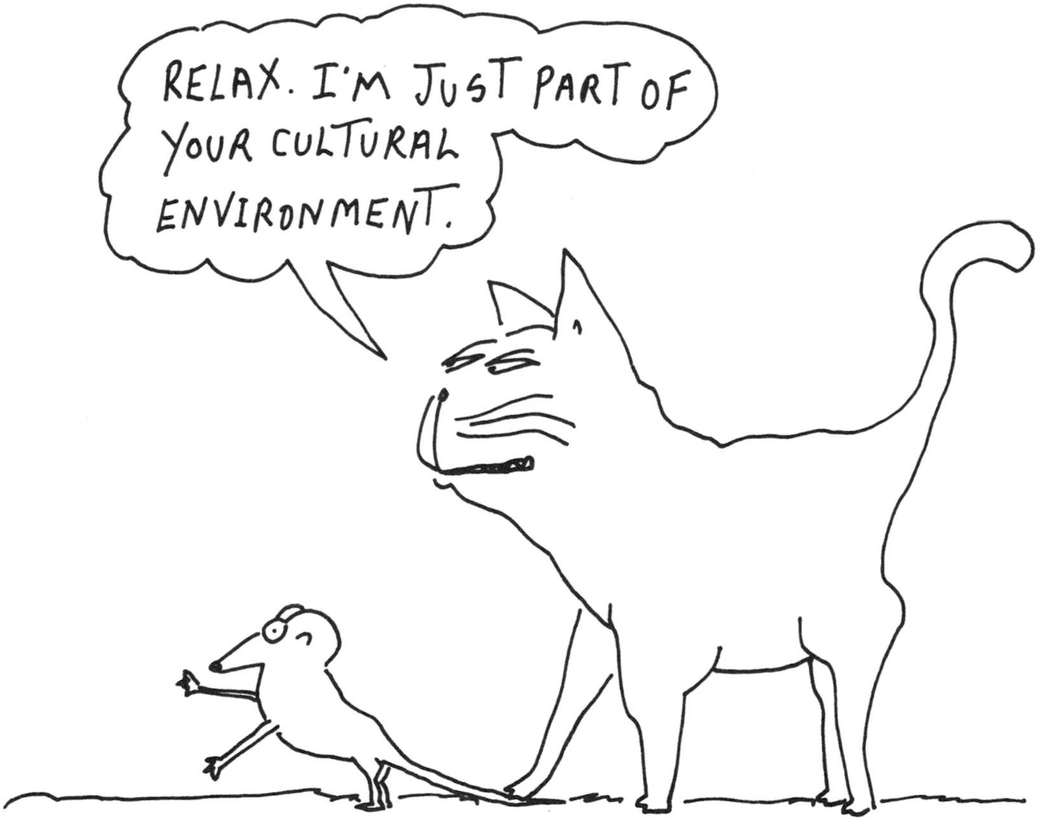
RELAX. I'M JUST PART OF YOUR CULTURAL ENVIRONMENT.

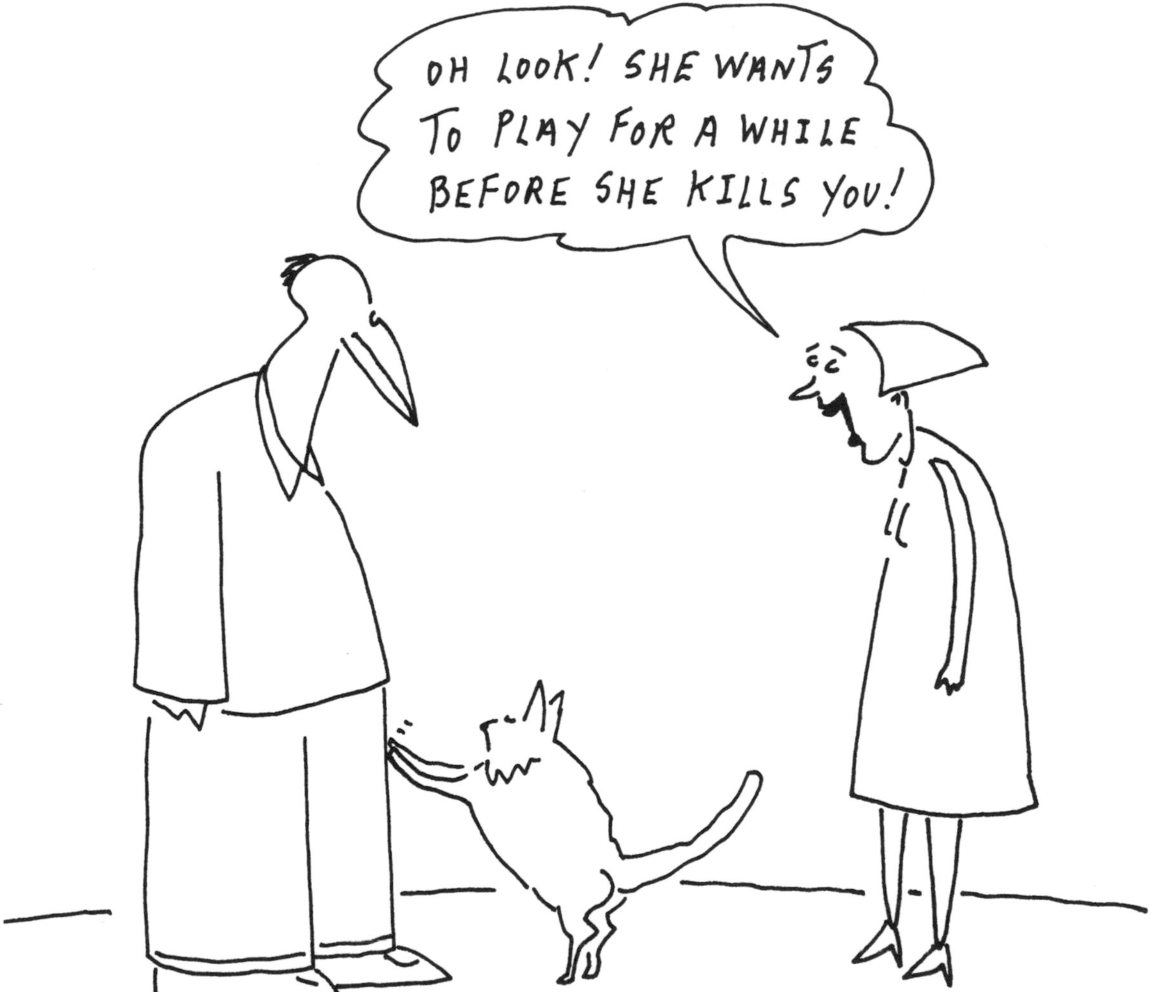
OH LOOK! SHE WANTS TO PLAY FOR A WHILE BEFORE SHE KILLS YOU!

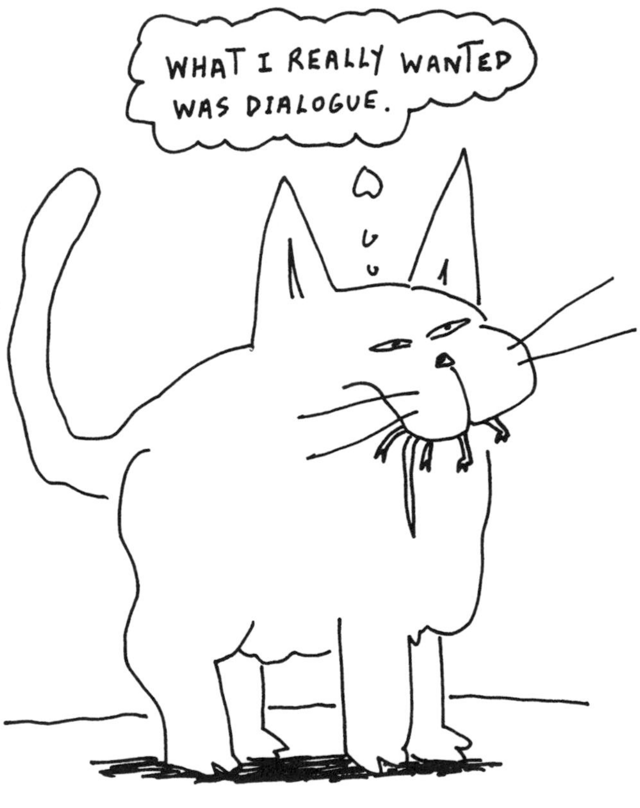
WHAT I REALLY WANTED WAS DIALOGUE.

ANTIDEPRESSANTS FOR KITTY

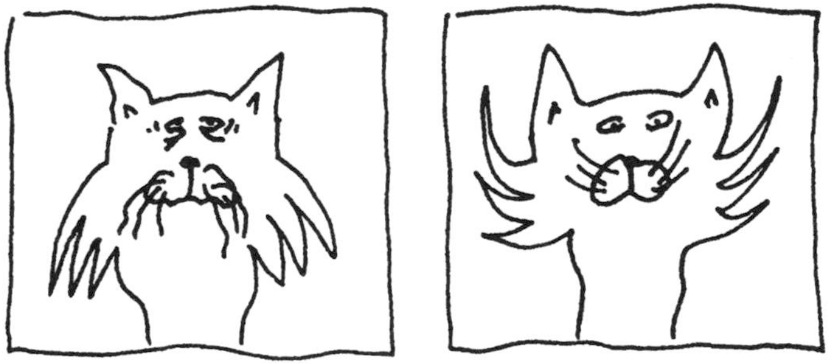

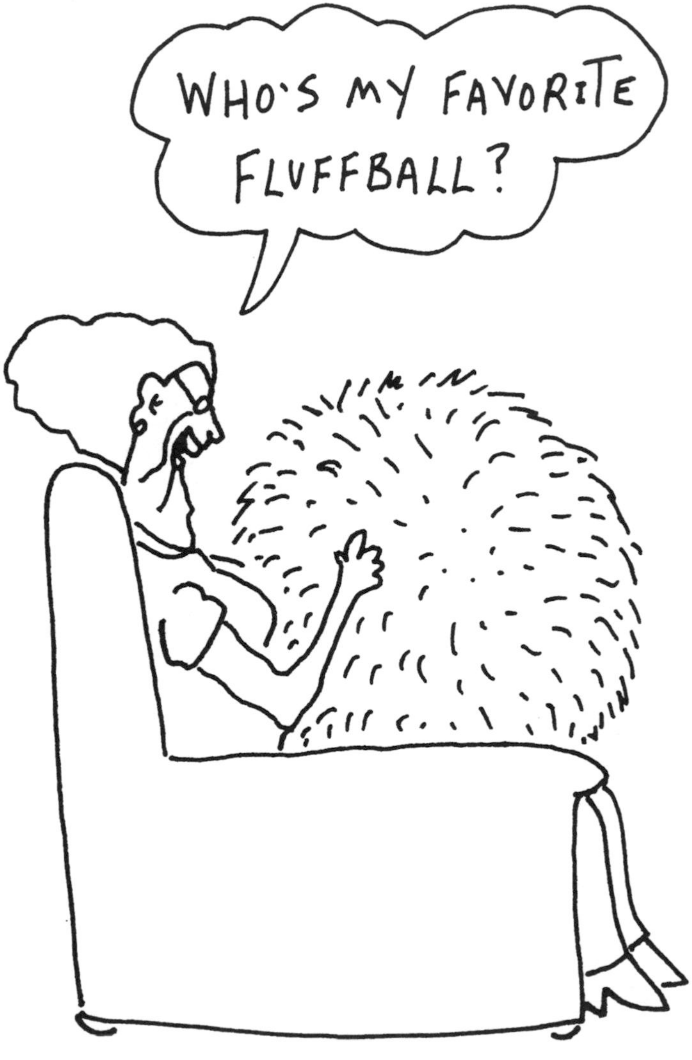
WHO'S MY FAVORITE FLUFFBALL?

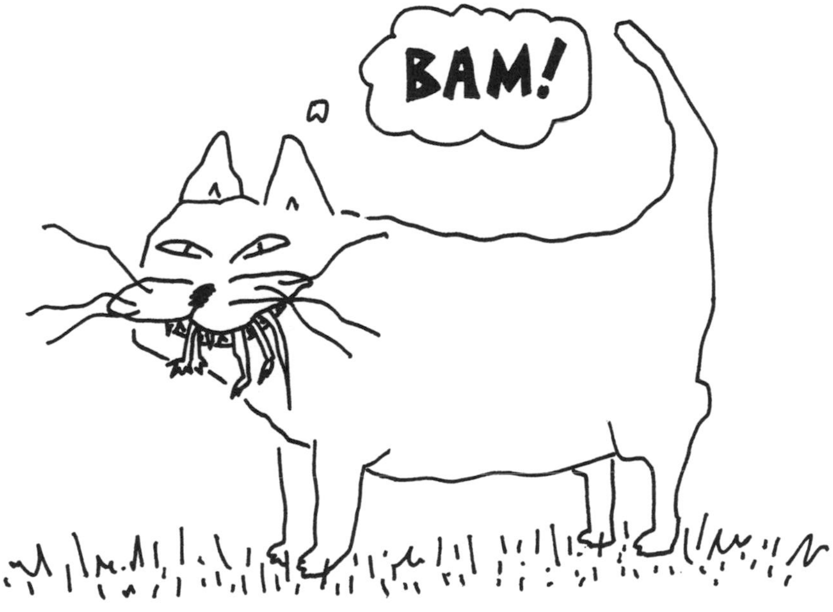
BAM!

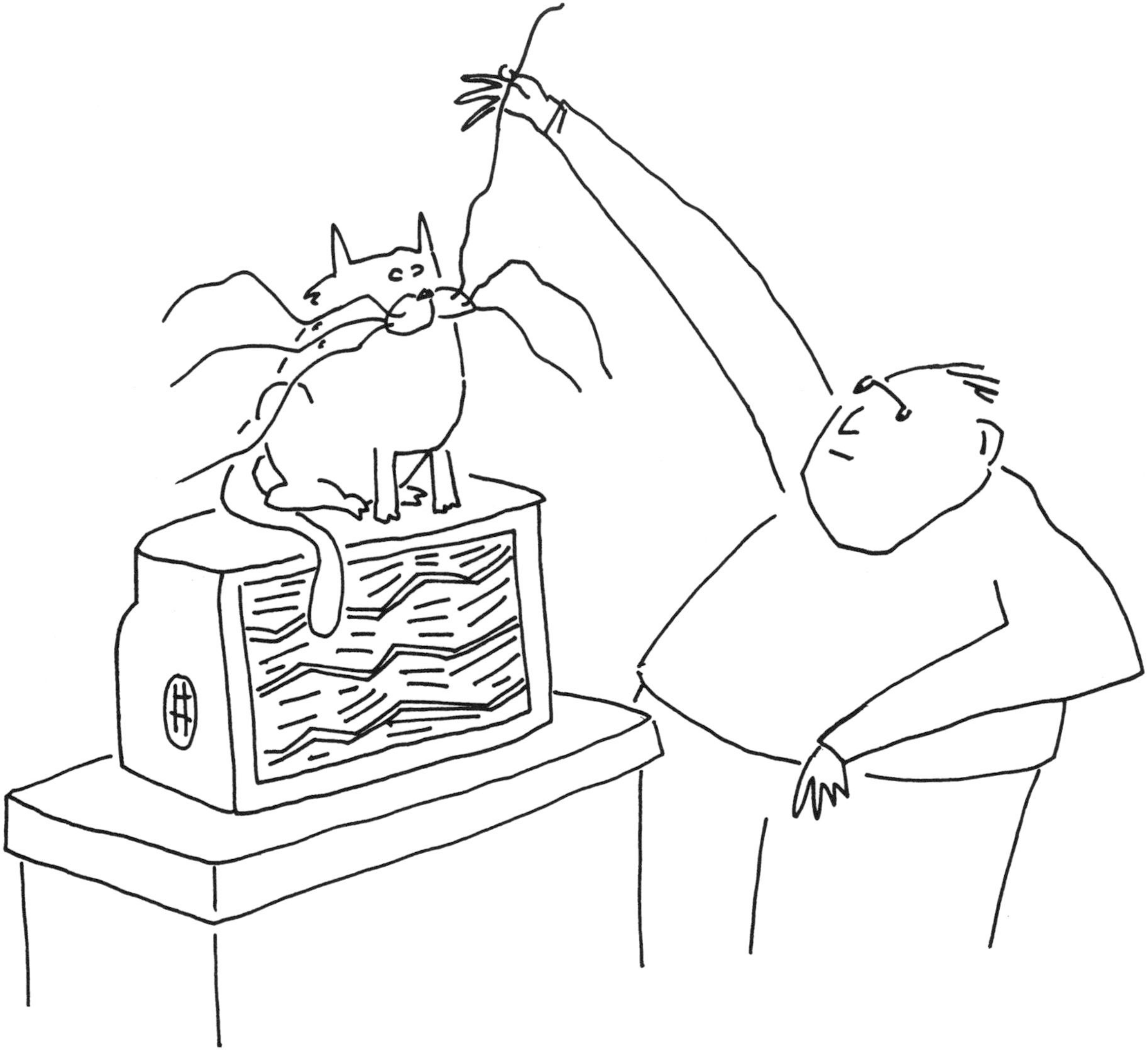

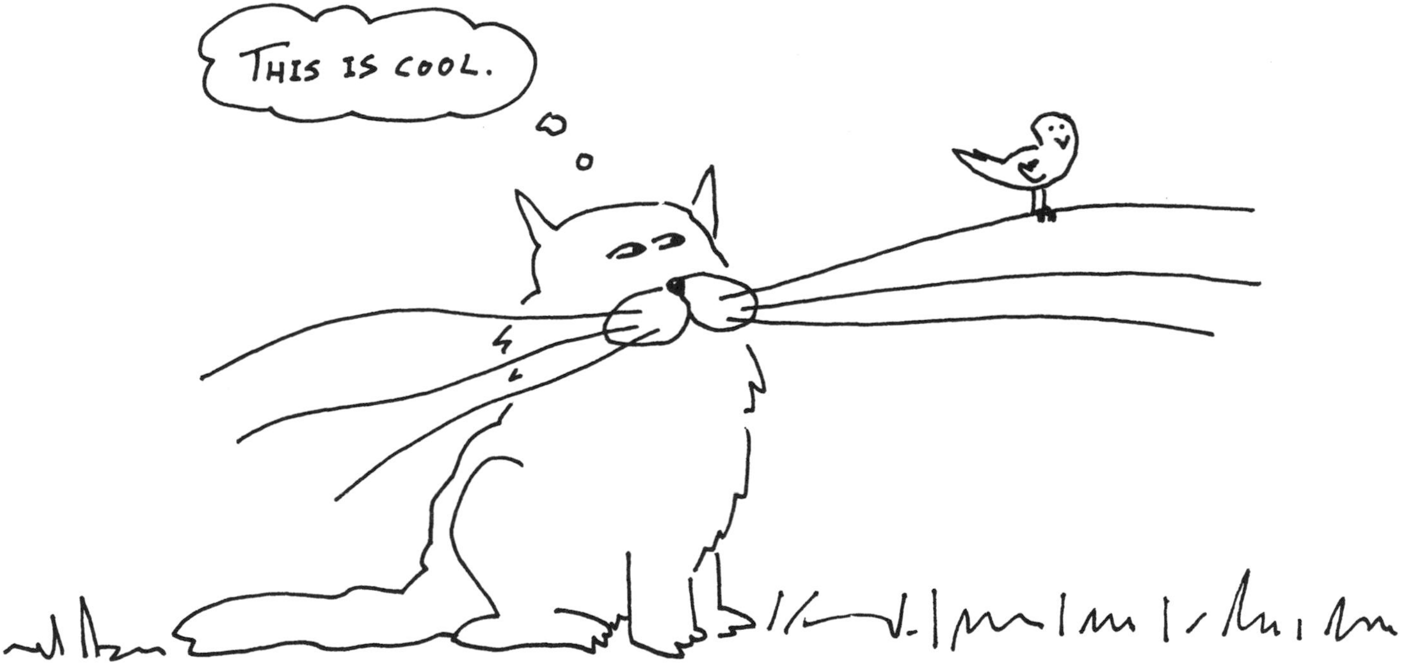
THIS IS COOL.

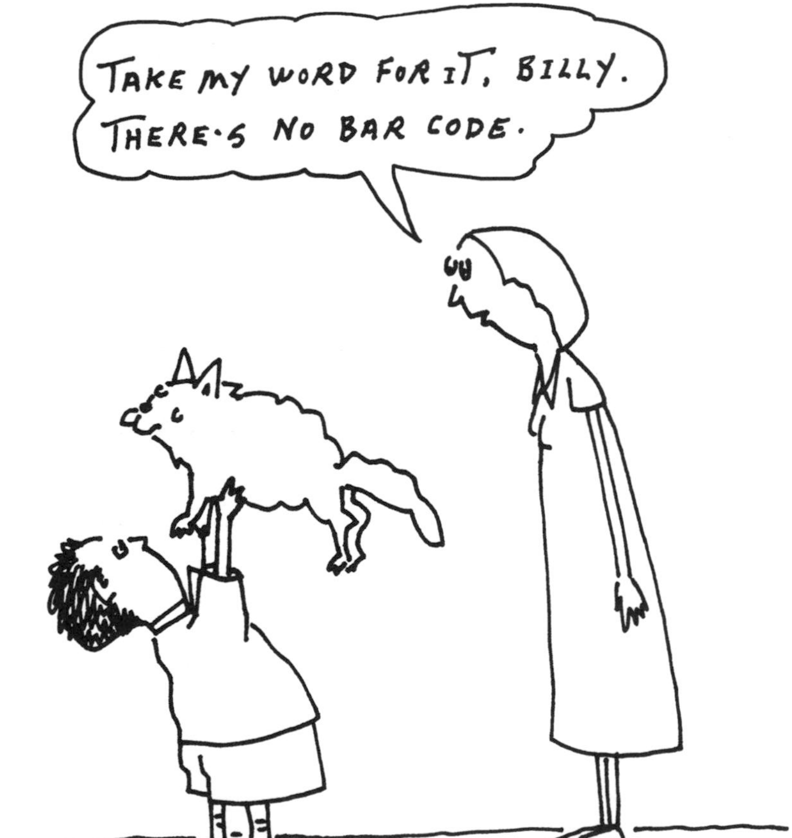
TAKE MY WORD FOR IT, BILLY.
THERE'S NO BAR CODE.

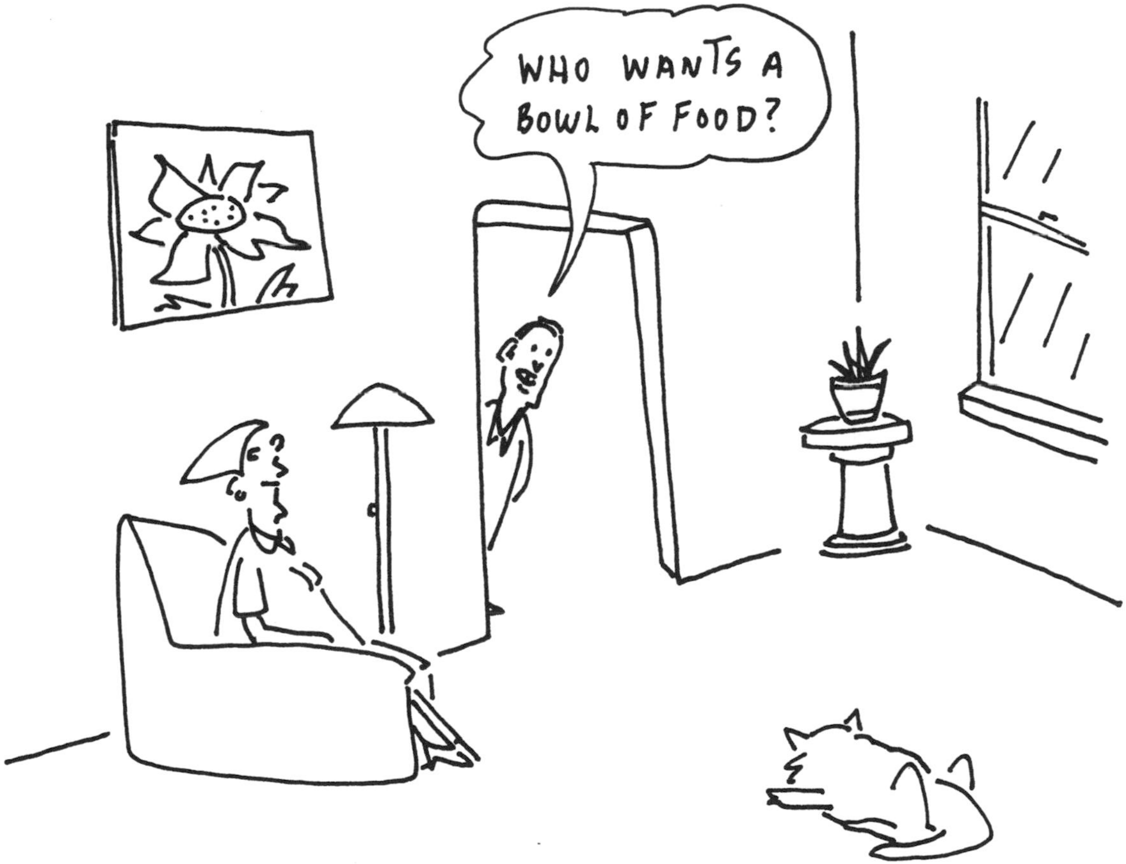
WHO WANTS A BOWL OF FOOD?

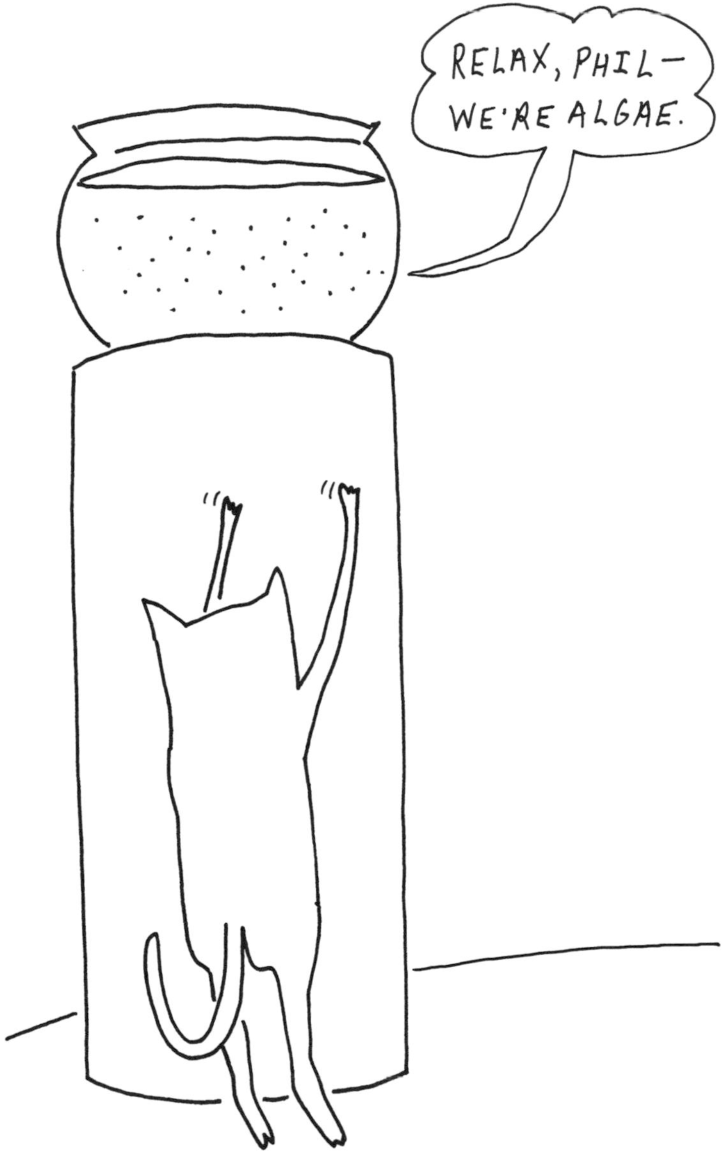
RELAX, PHIL—
WE'RE ALGAE.

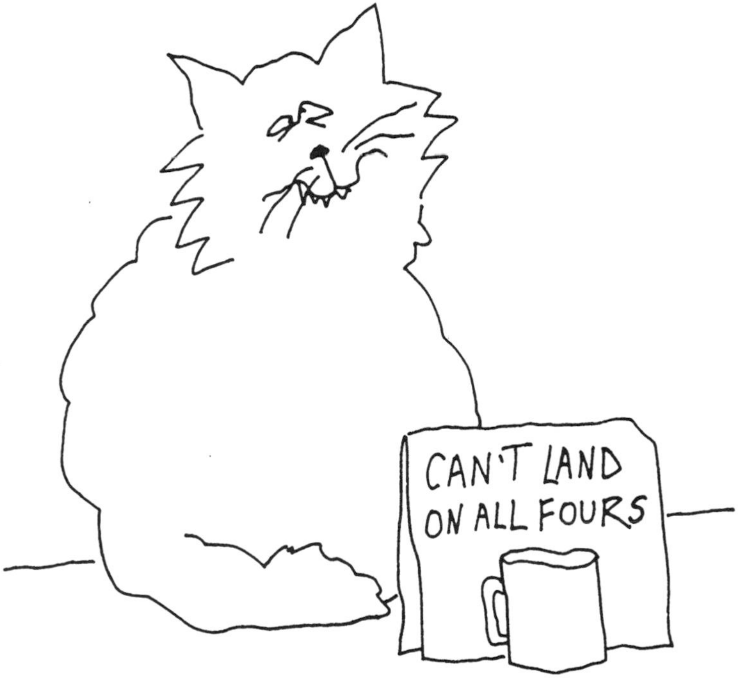
CAN'T LAND
ON ALL FOURS

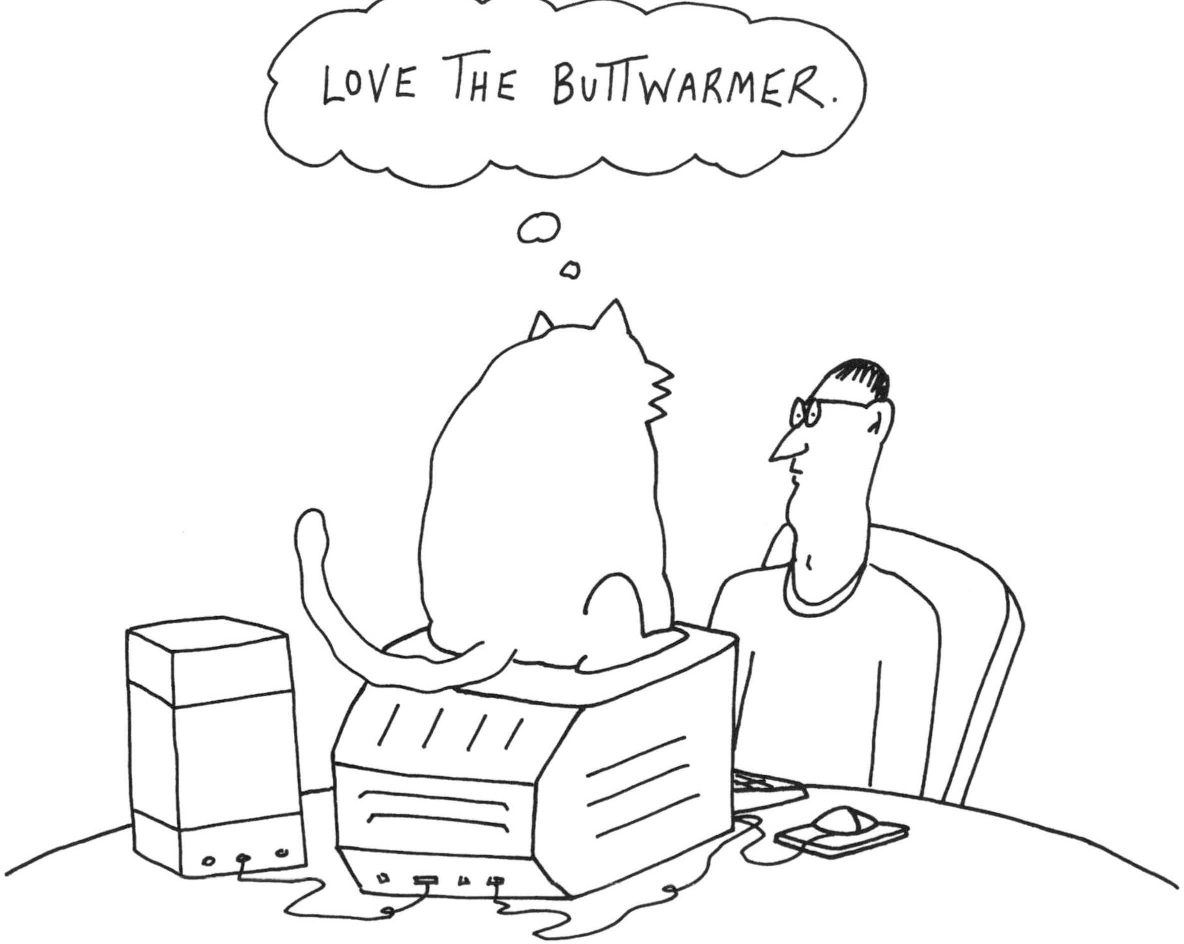
LOVE THE BUTTWARMER.

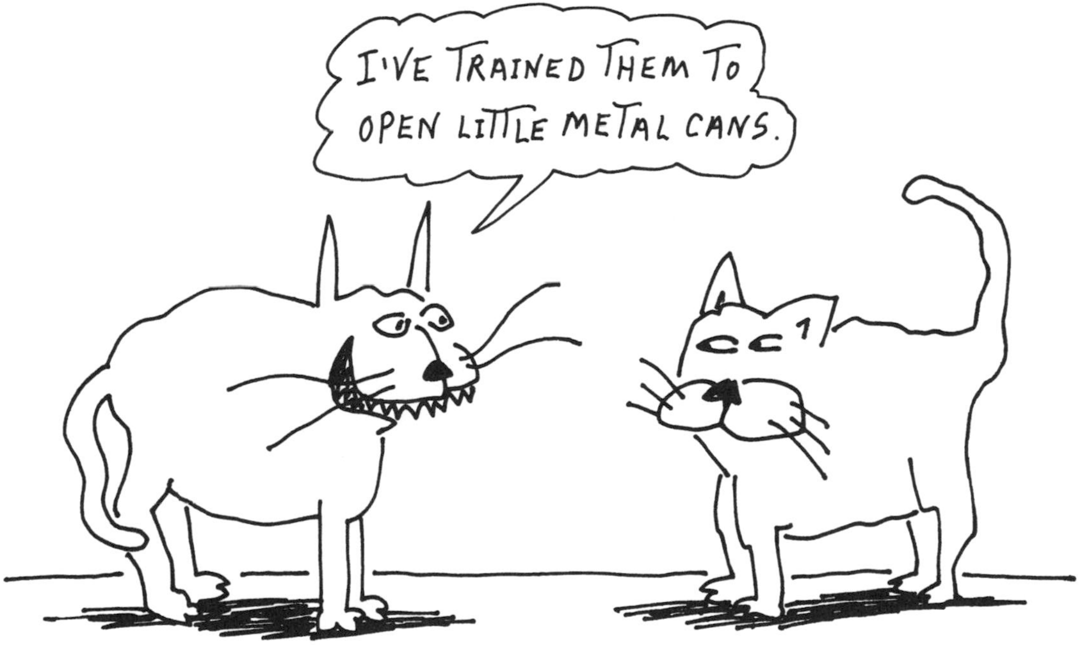
I'VE TRAINED THEM TO OPEN LITTLE METAL CANS.

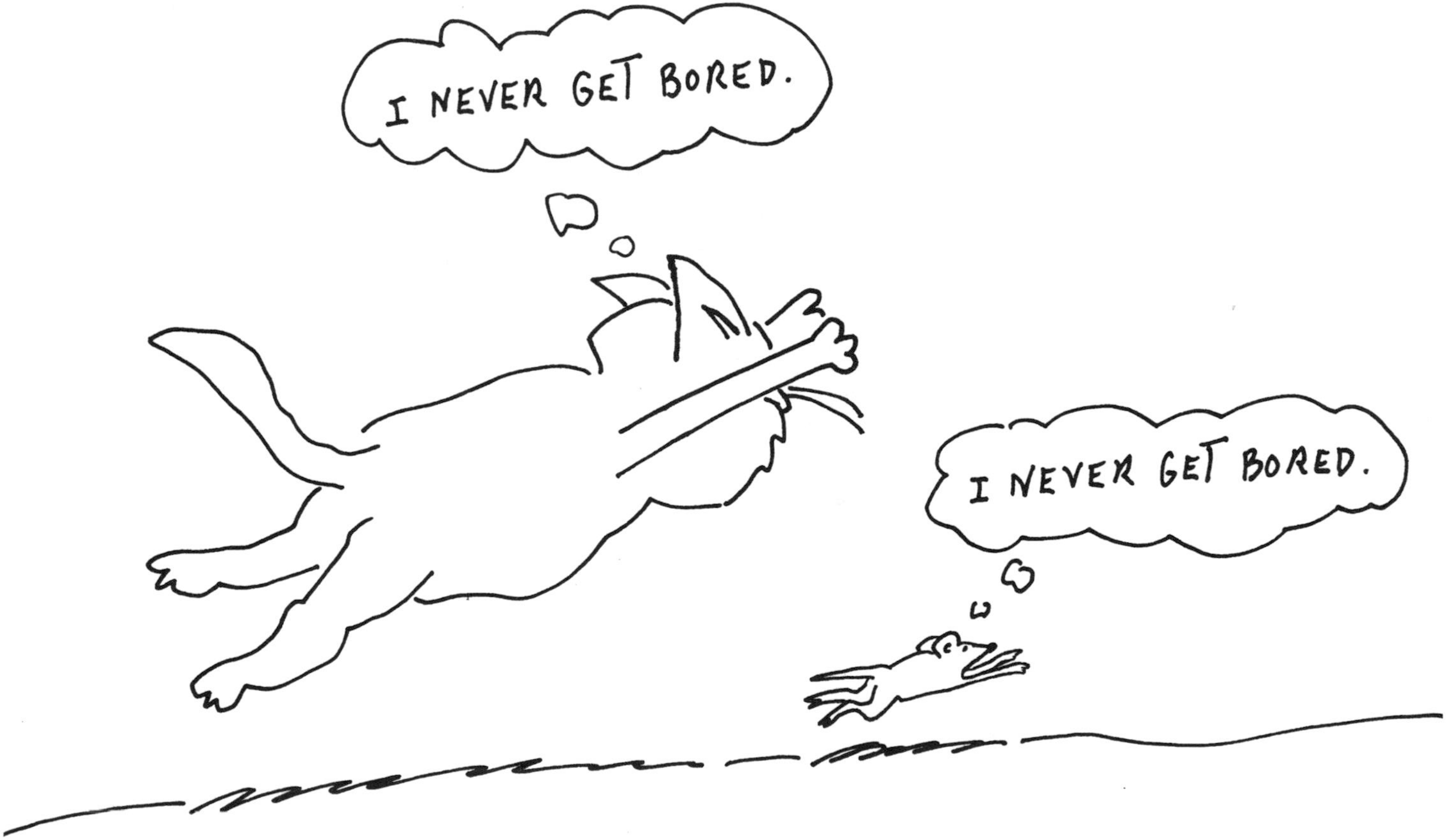
I NEVER GET BORED.
I NEVER GET BORED.

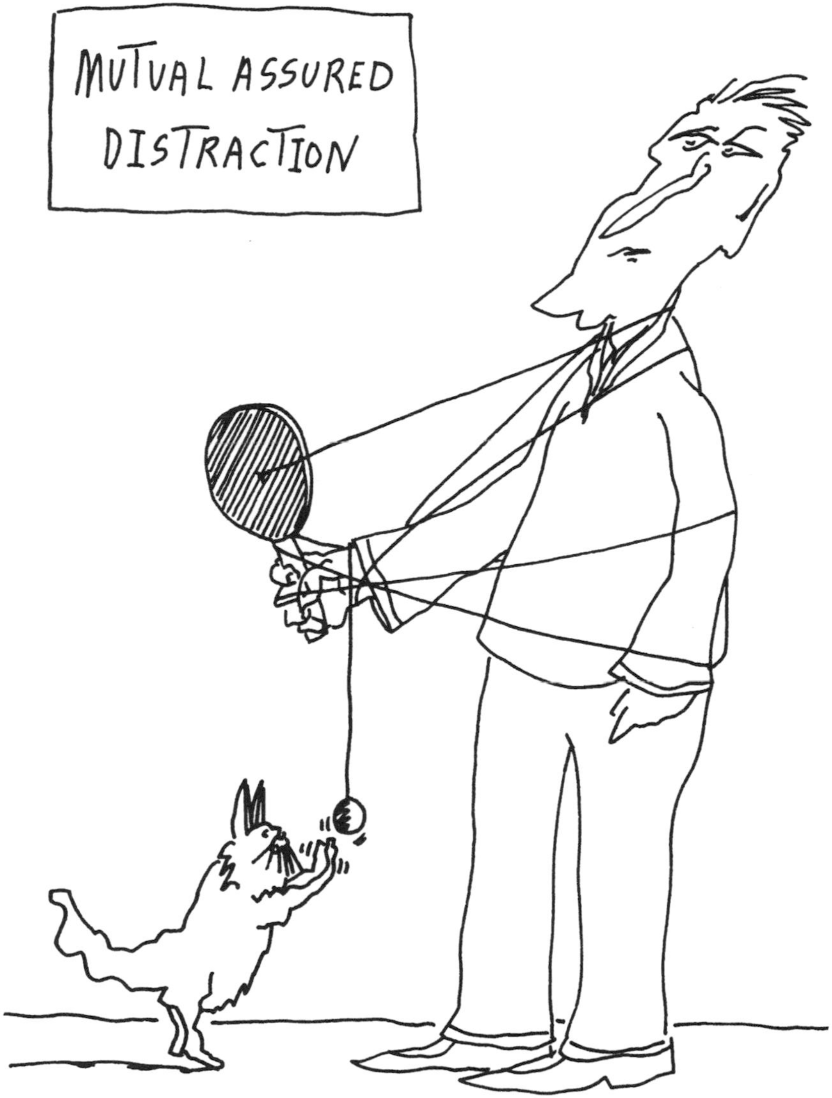
MUTUAL ASSURED DISTRACTION

THE HAIR CLUB FOR CAT LOVERS

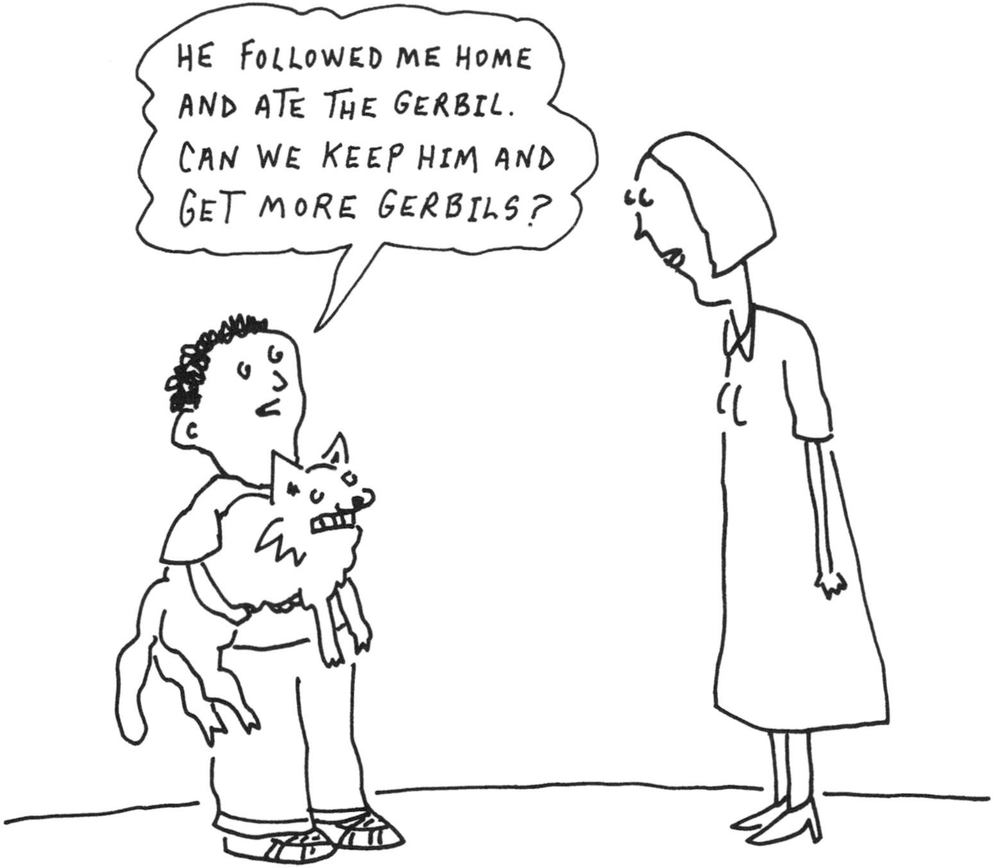
HE FOLLOWED ME HOME AND ATE THE GERBIL. CAN WE KEEP HIM AND GET MORE GERBILS?

# HIGH MAINTENANCE KITTY

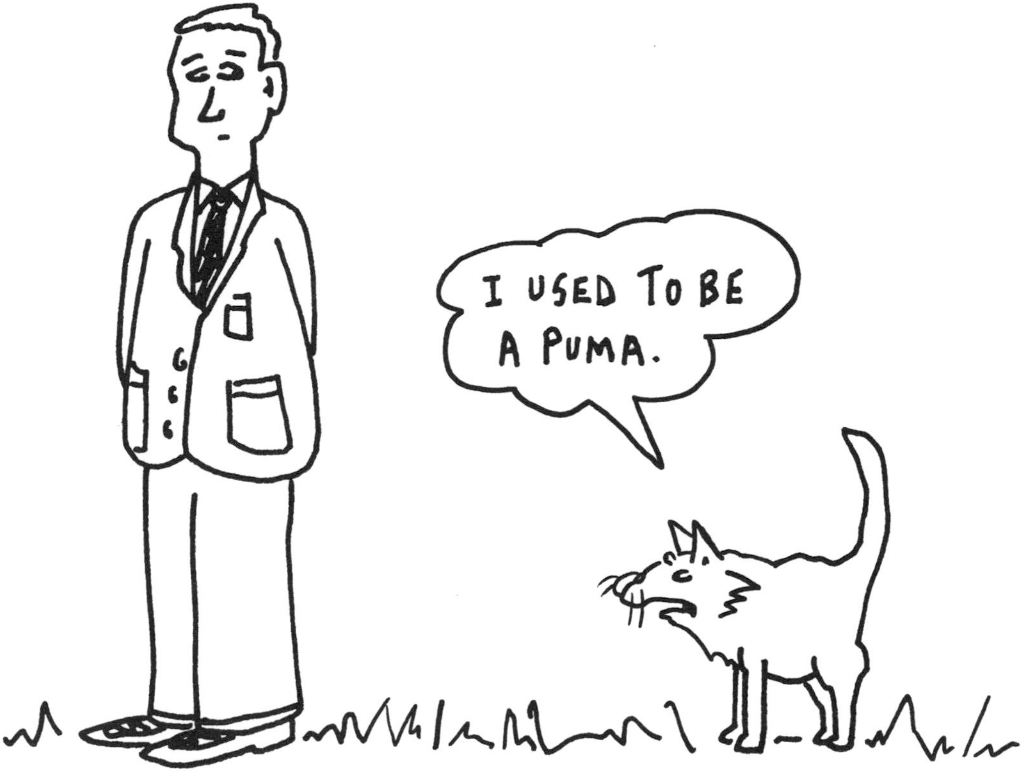
I USED TO BE A PUMA.

DOWNSIZING IN NATURE

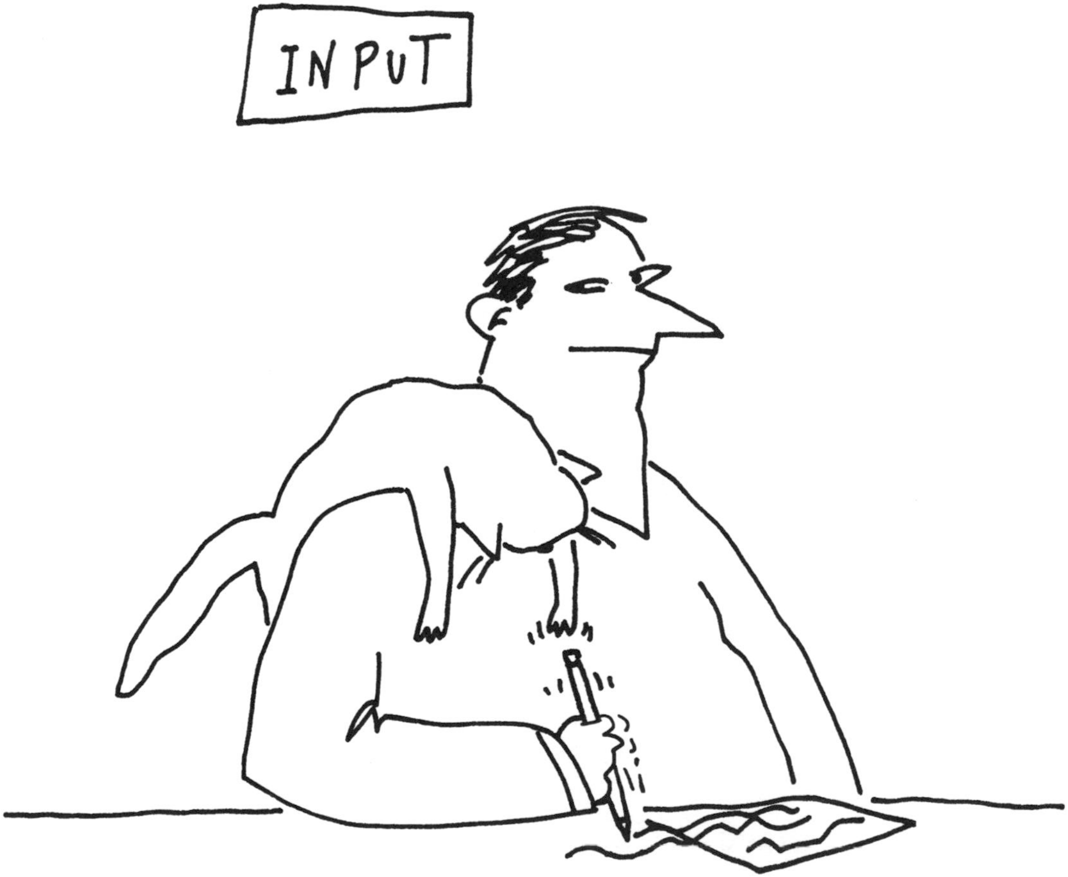
INPUT

JO JO THE DOG-FACED BOY
AFTER CORRECTIVE SURGERY

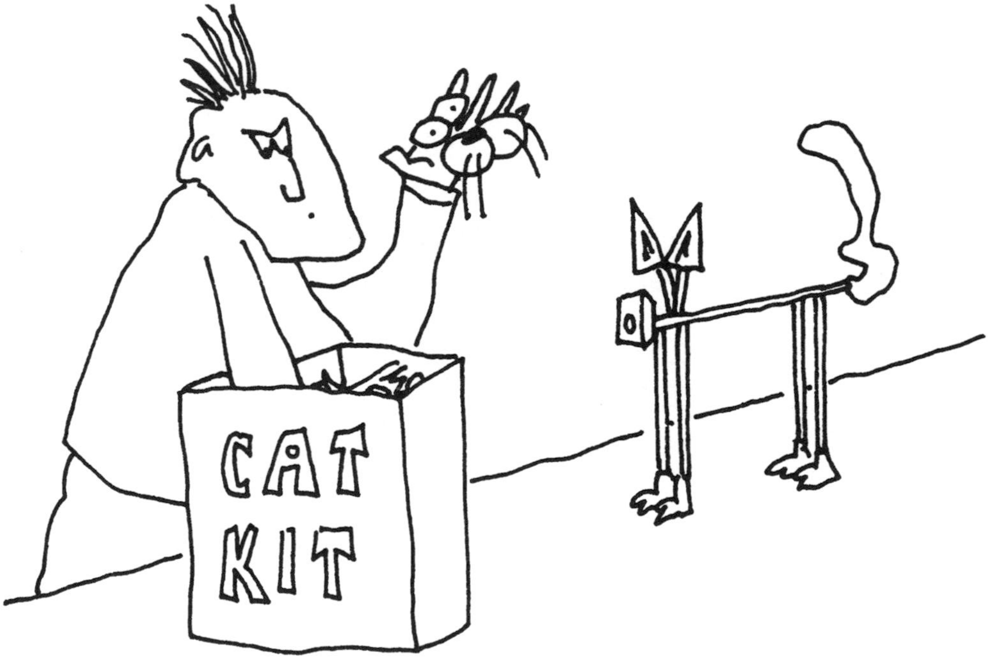
CAT KIT

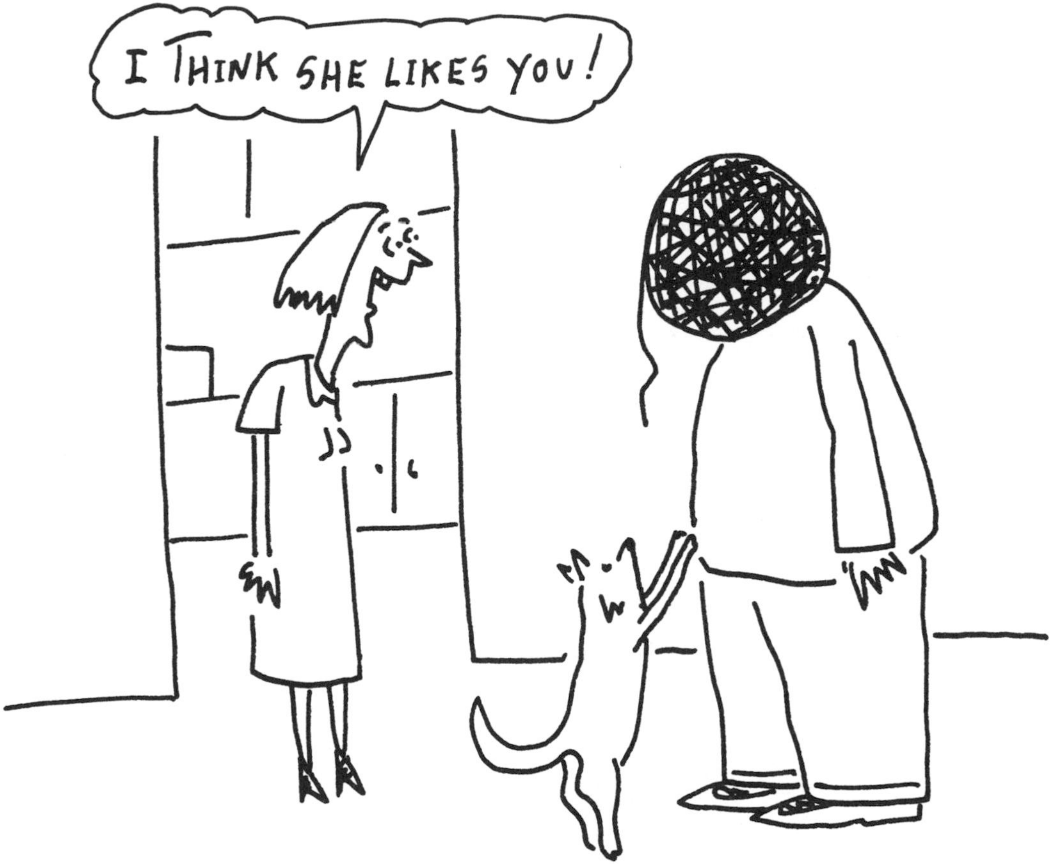
I THINK SHE LIKES YOU!

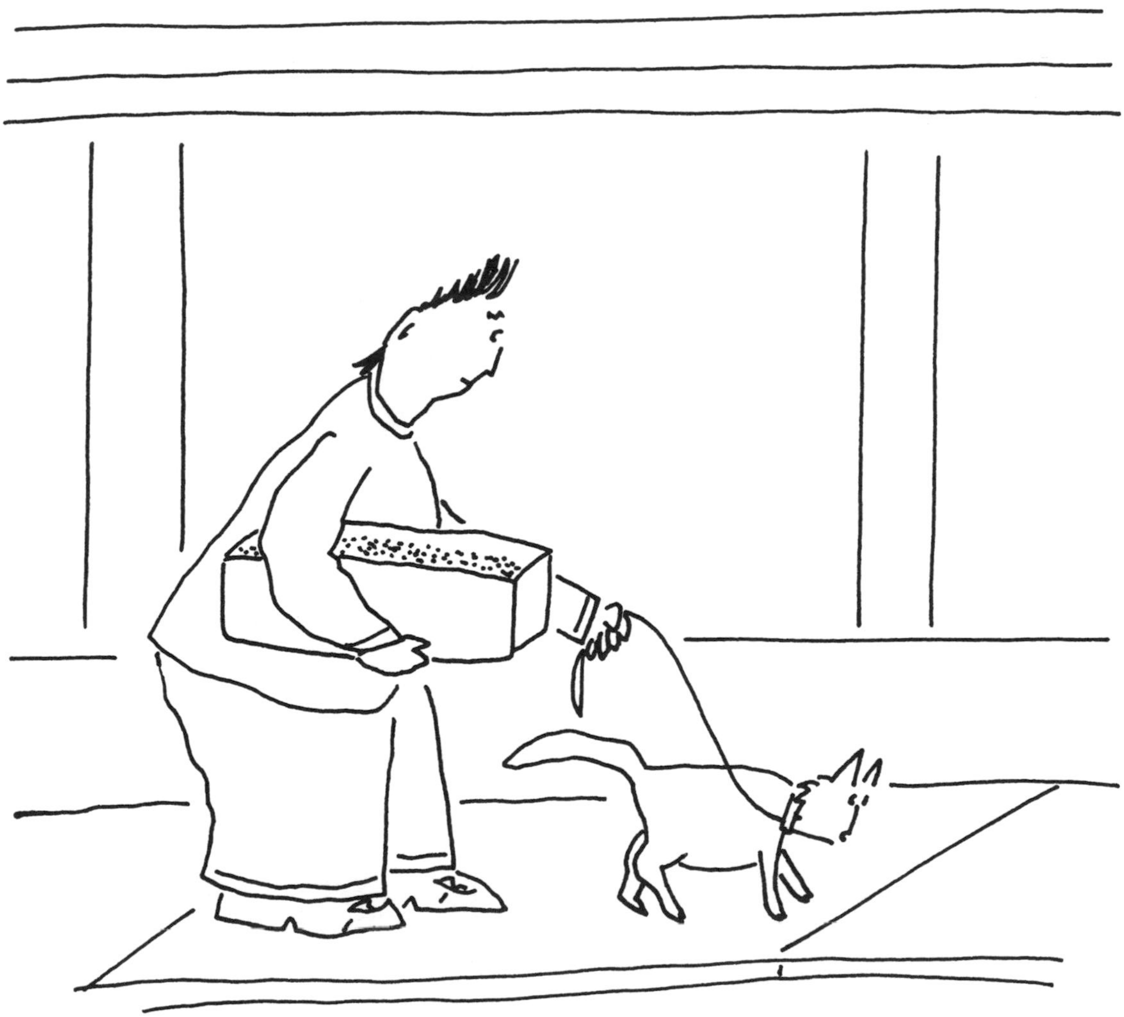

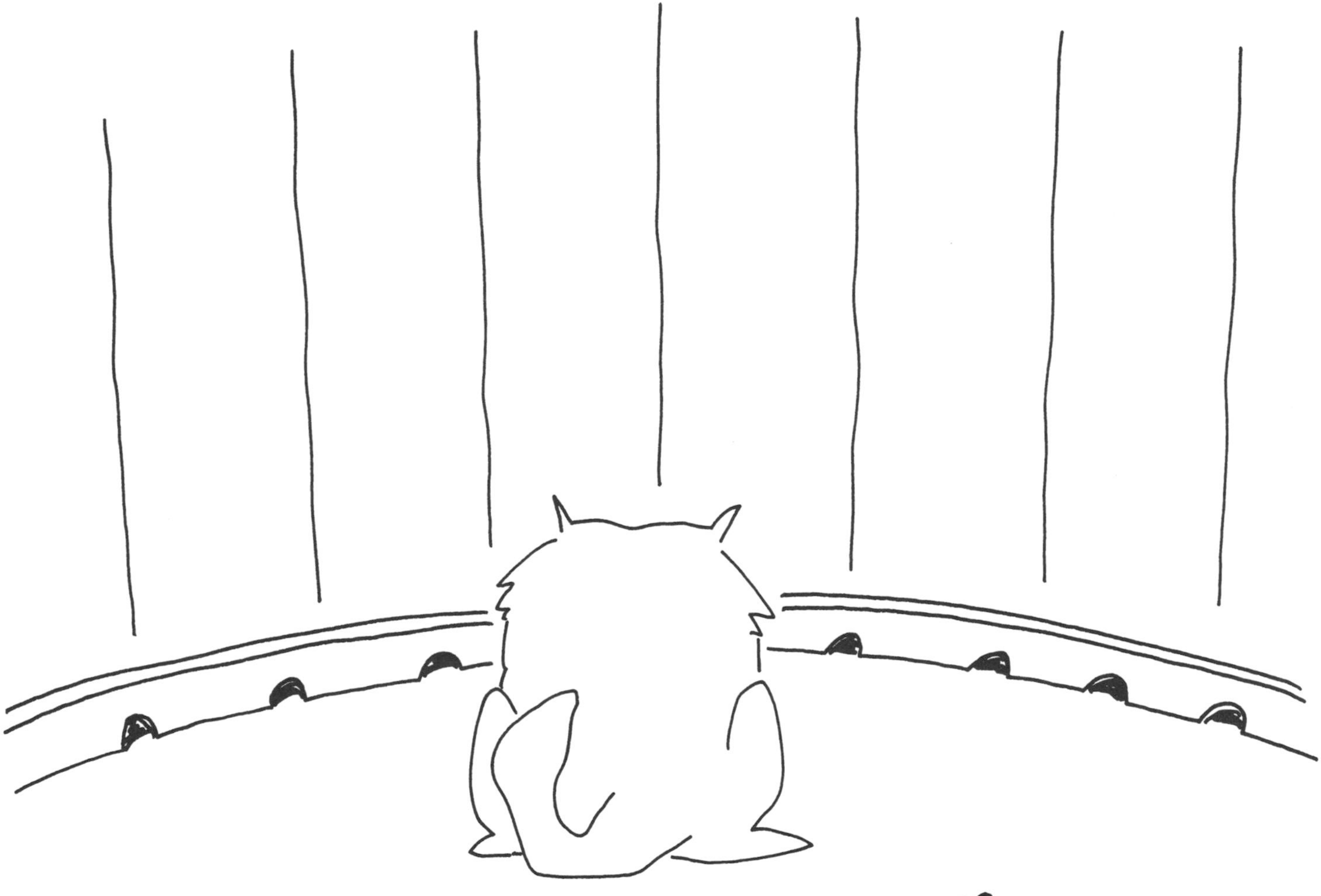

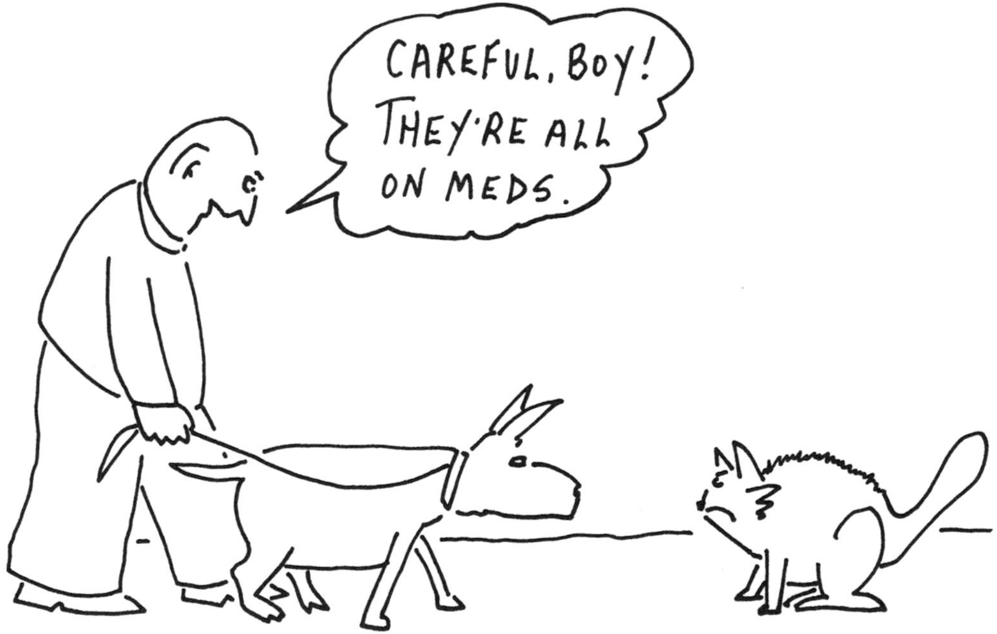
CAREFUL, BOY! THEY'RE ALL ON MEDS.

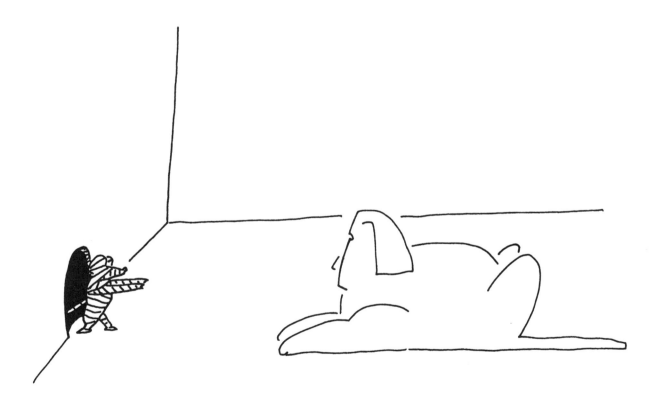

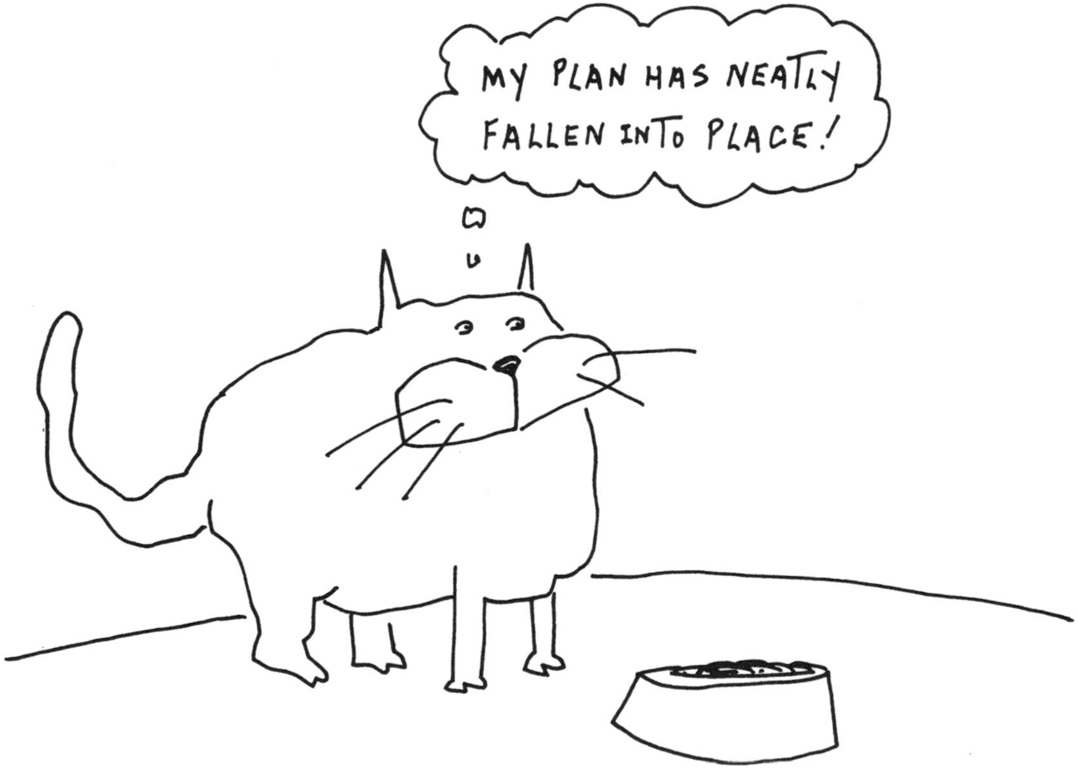
MY PLAN HAS NEATLY FALLEN INTO PLACE!

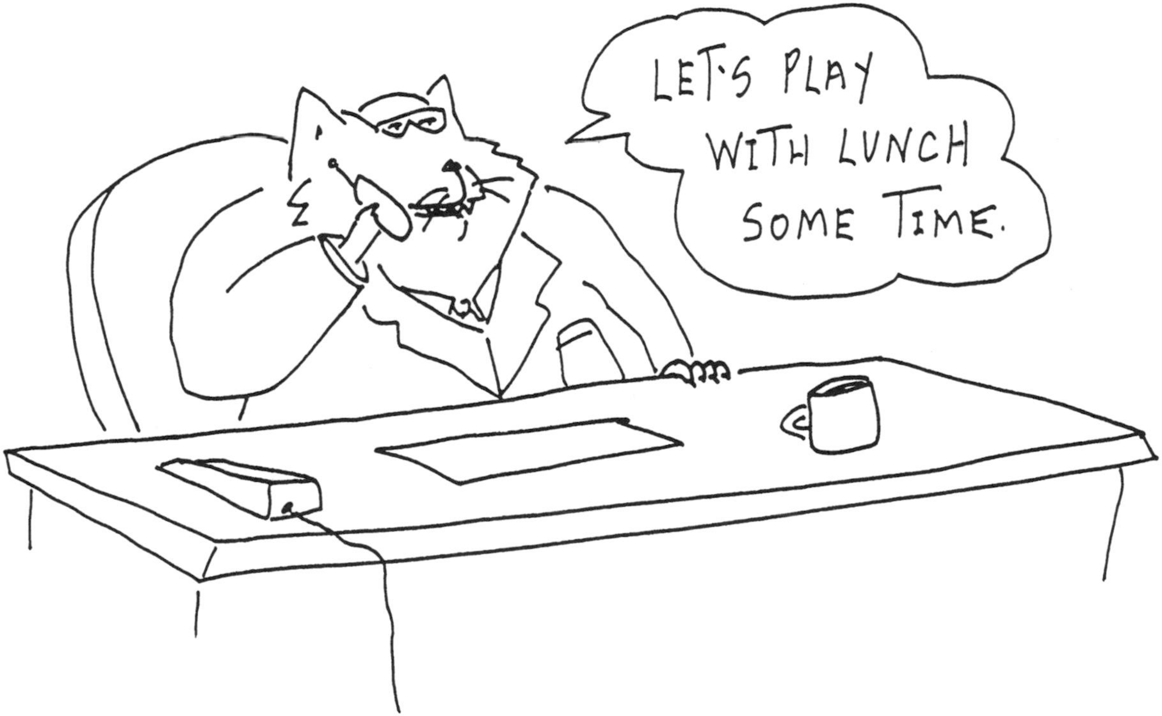
LET'S PLAY WITH LUNCH SOME TIME.

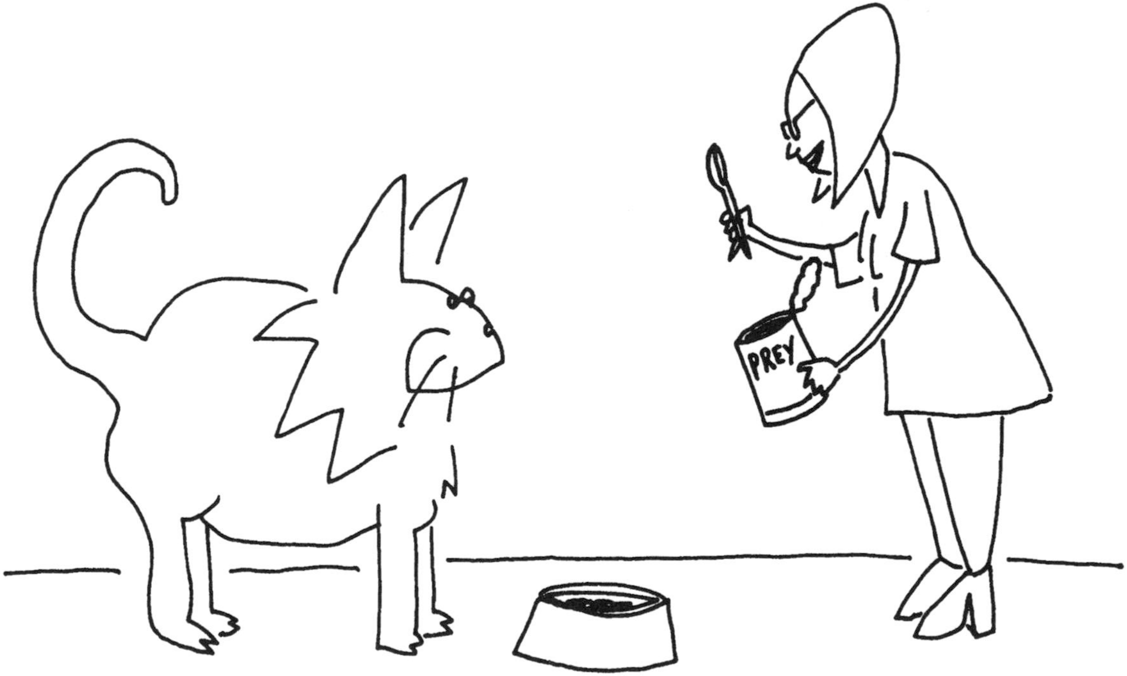
PREY

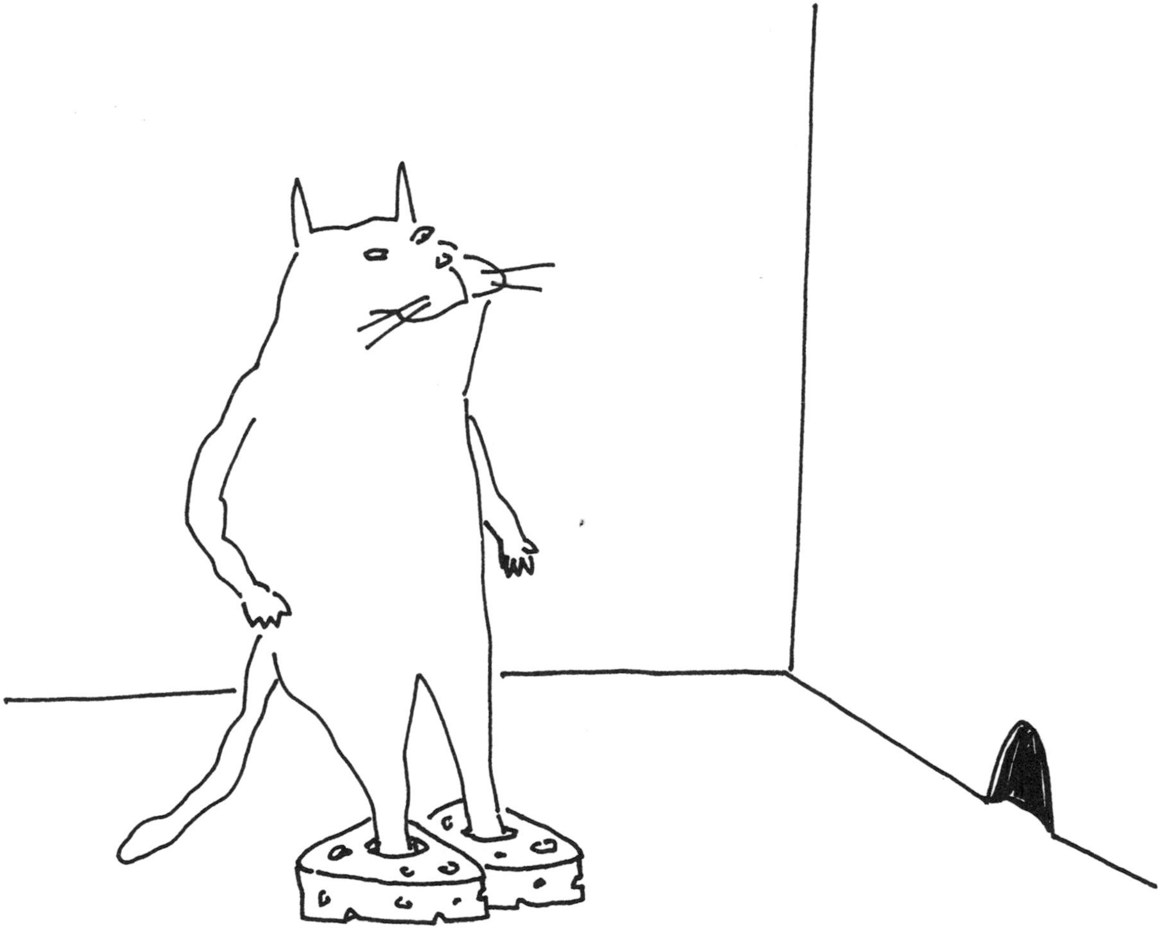

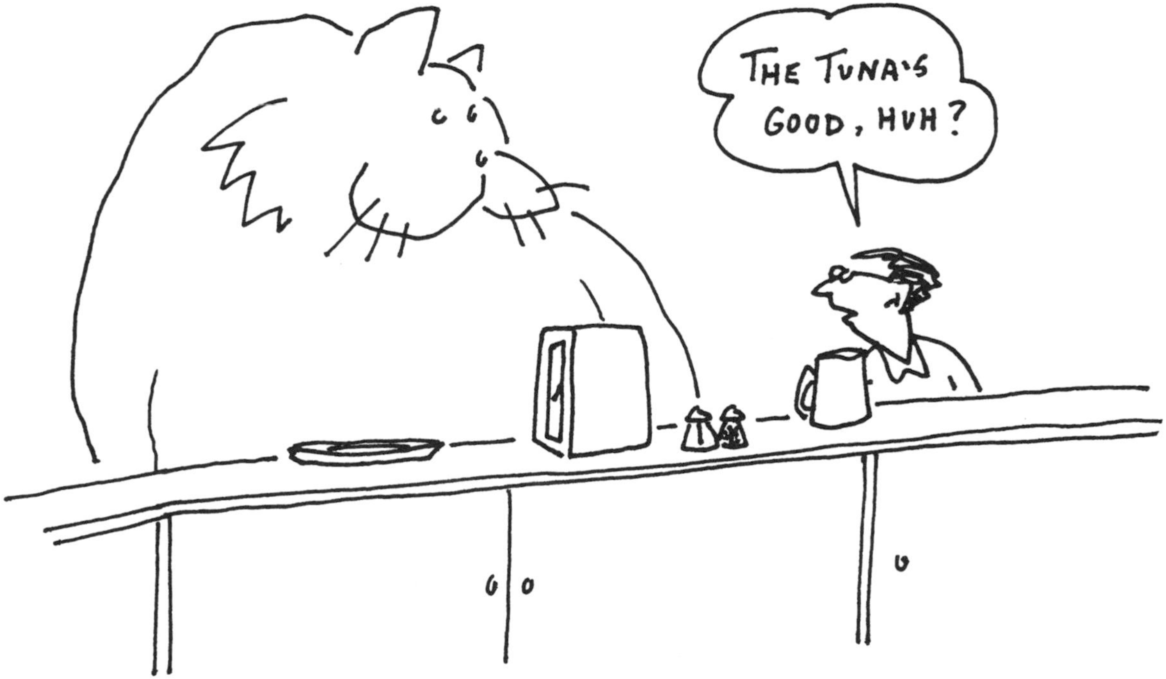
THE TUNA'S GOOD, HUH?

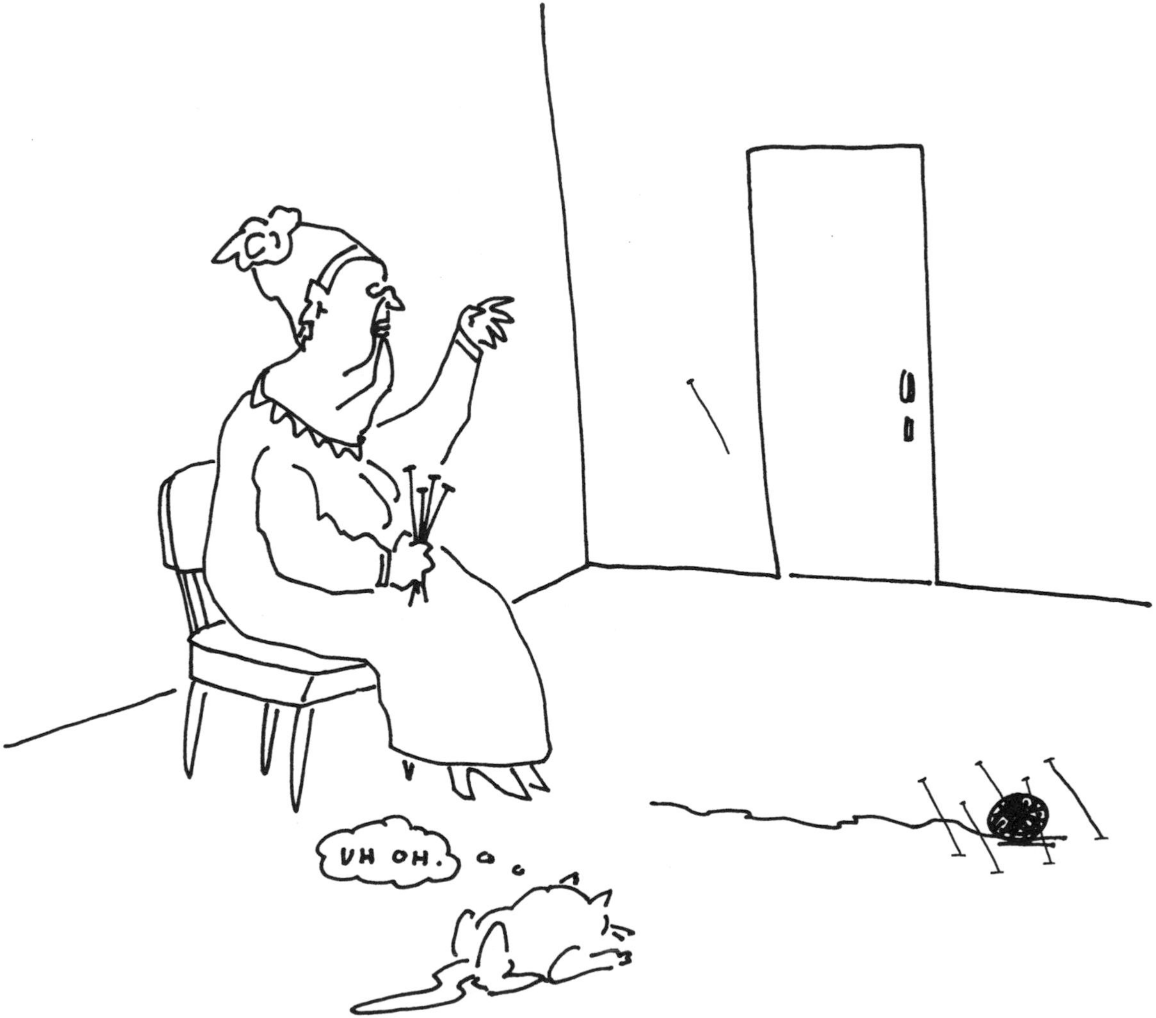
UH OH.

# KITTYCLOPS

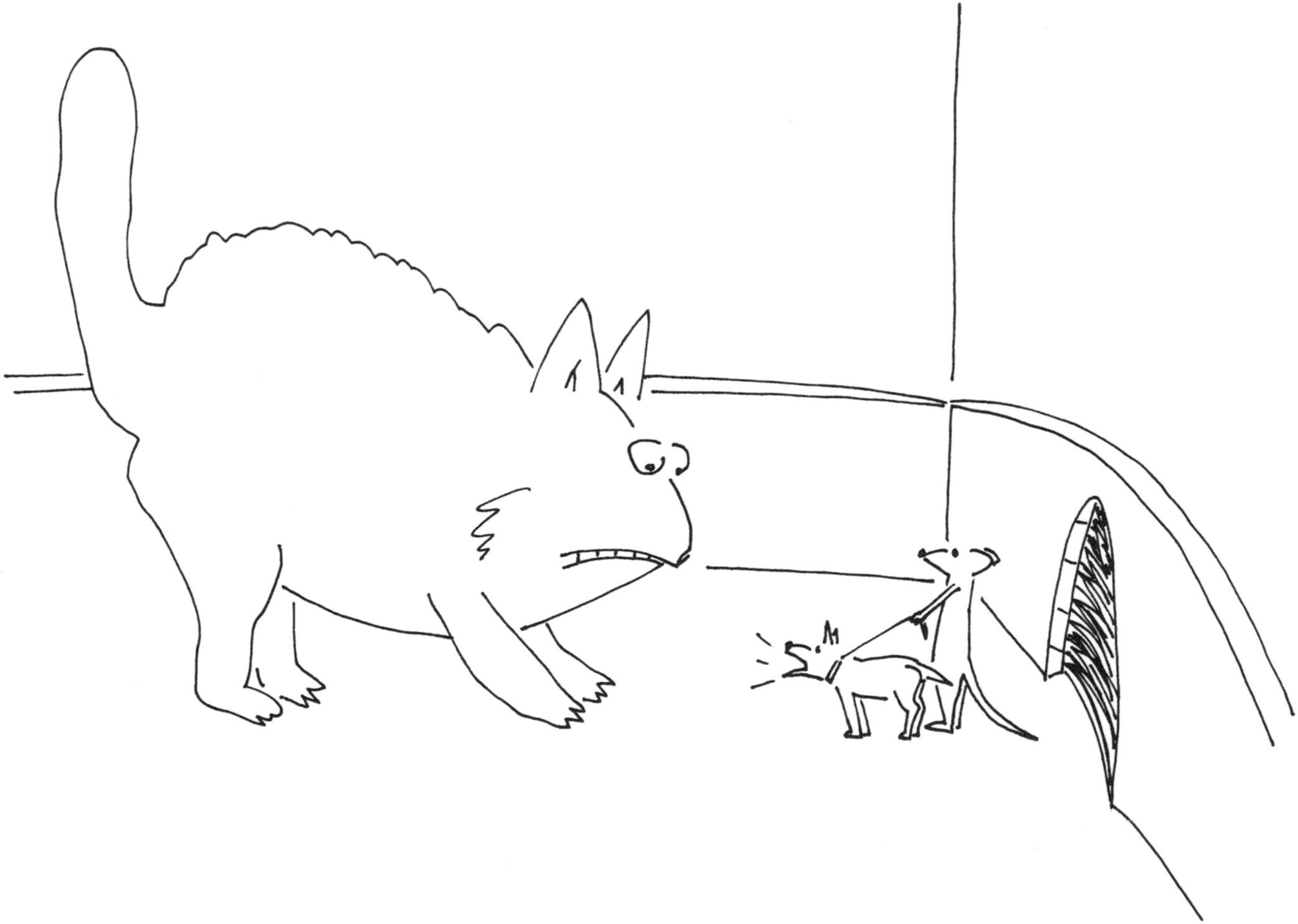

# Dogs
## and
# Cats

P.S. MUELLER

**JONES BOOKS** • MADISON WISCONSIN USA

*To my brother*
*Jim*

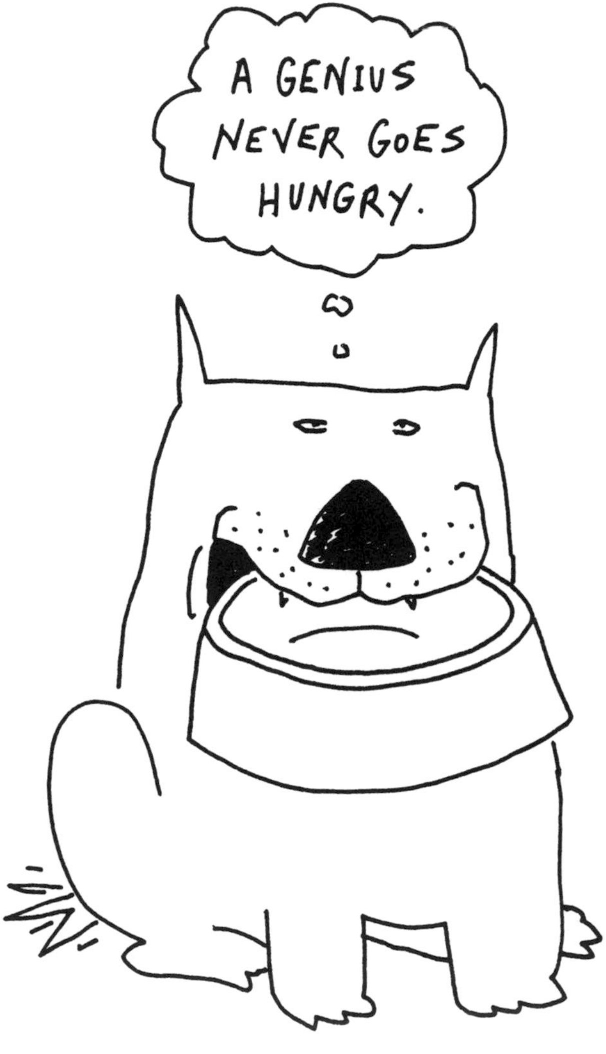
A GENIUS NEVER GOES HUNGRY.

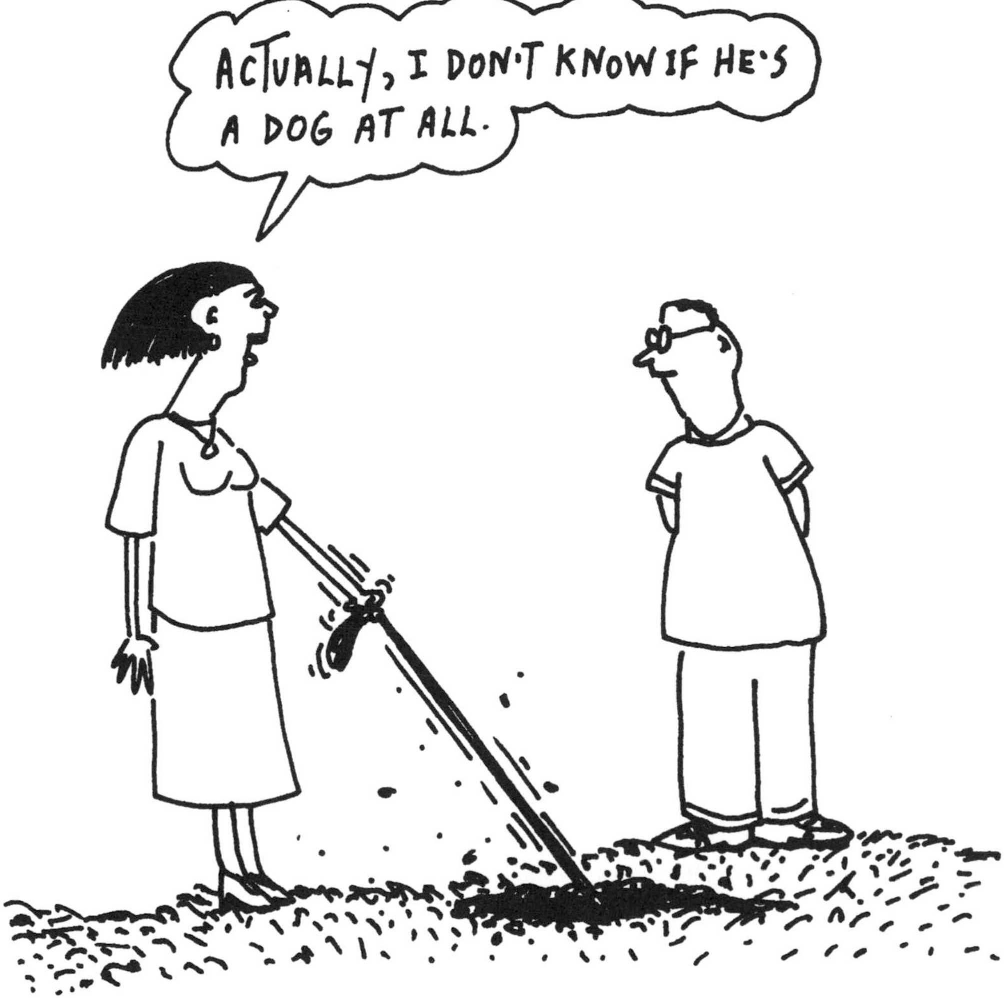
ACTUALLY, I DON'T KNOW IF HE'S A DOG AT ALL.

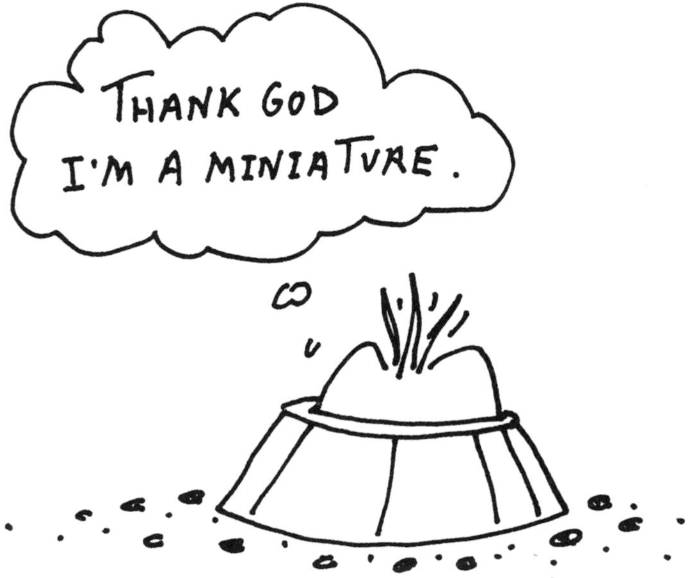
THANK GOD
I'M A MINIATURE.

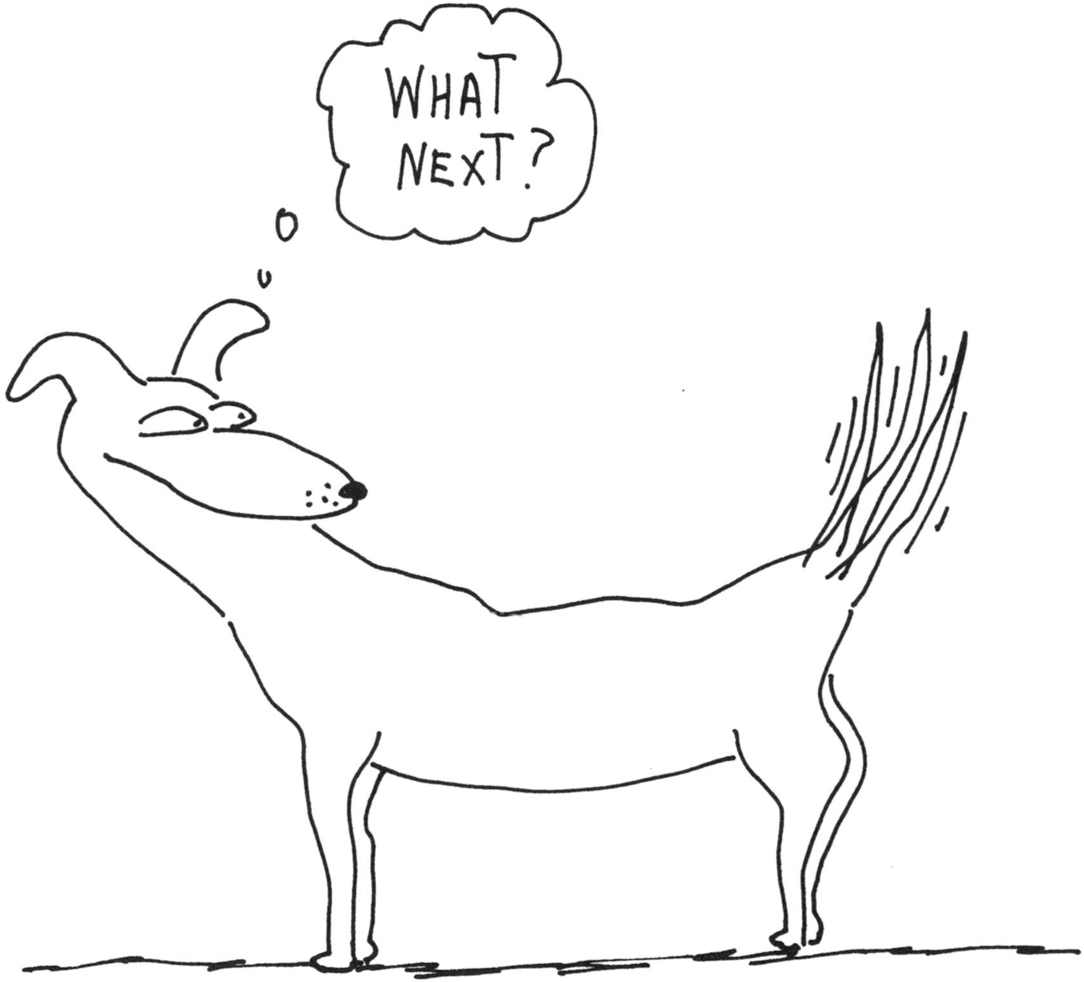
WHAT NEXT?

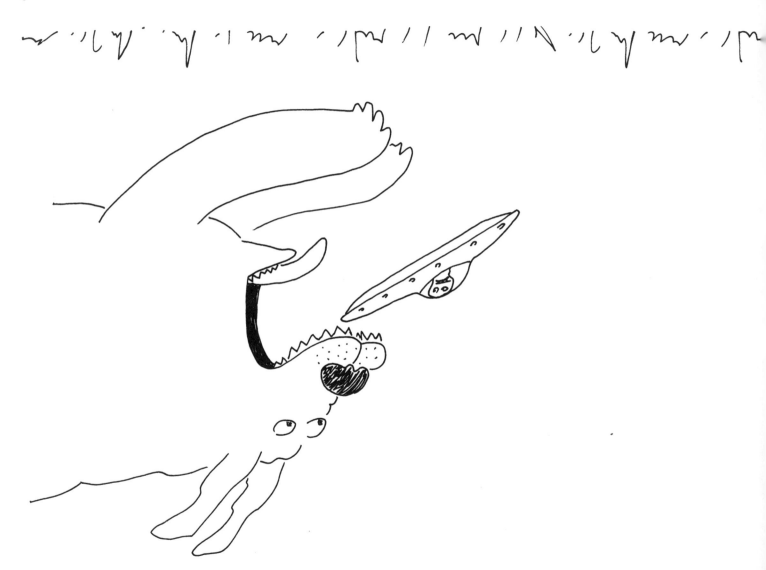

SOONER OR LATER
THE FREE RIDE
WILL END.

THE DARKNESS OF PRINCE

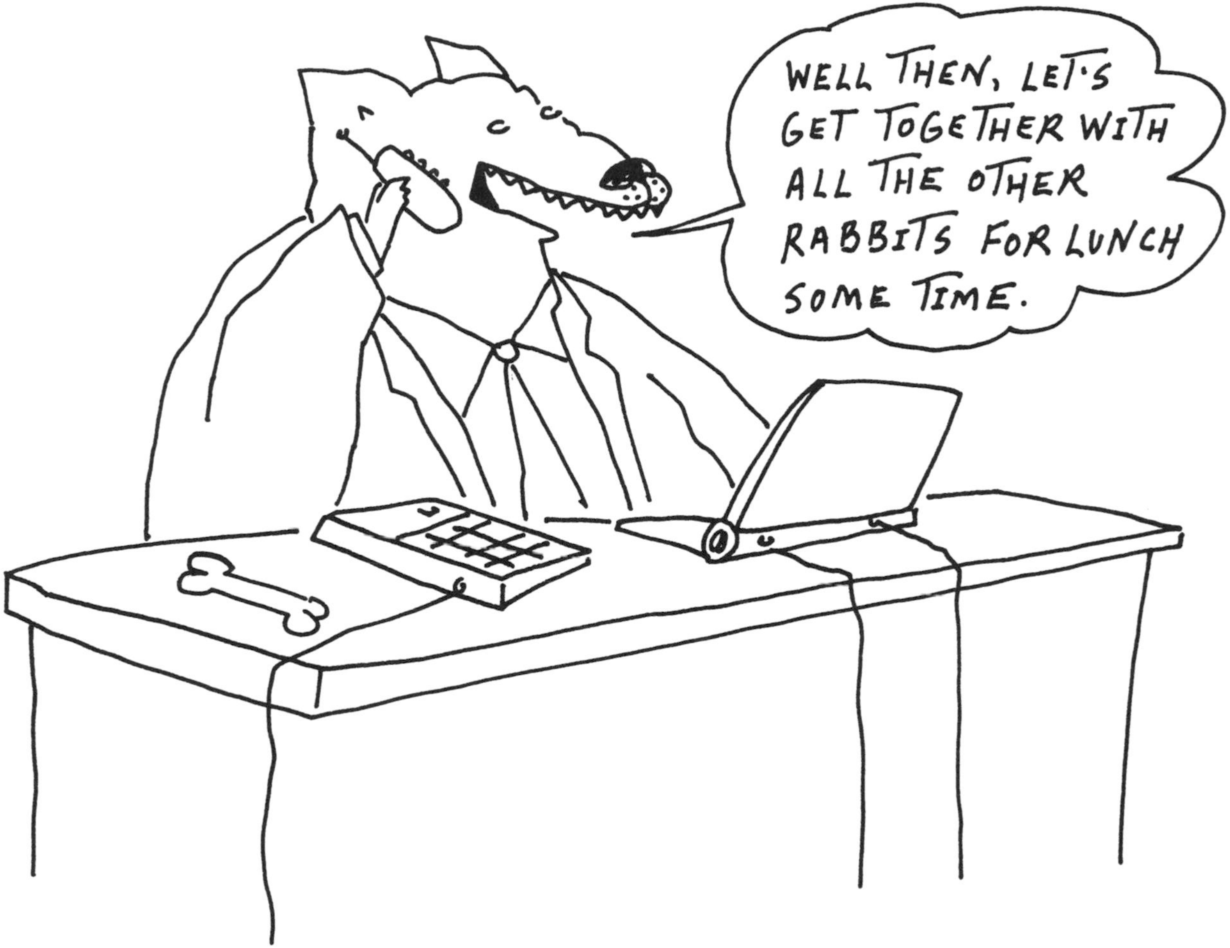
WELL THEN, LET'S GET TOGETHER WITH ALL THE OTHER RABBITS FOR LUNCH SOME TIME.

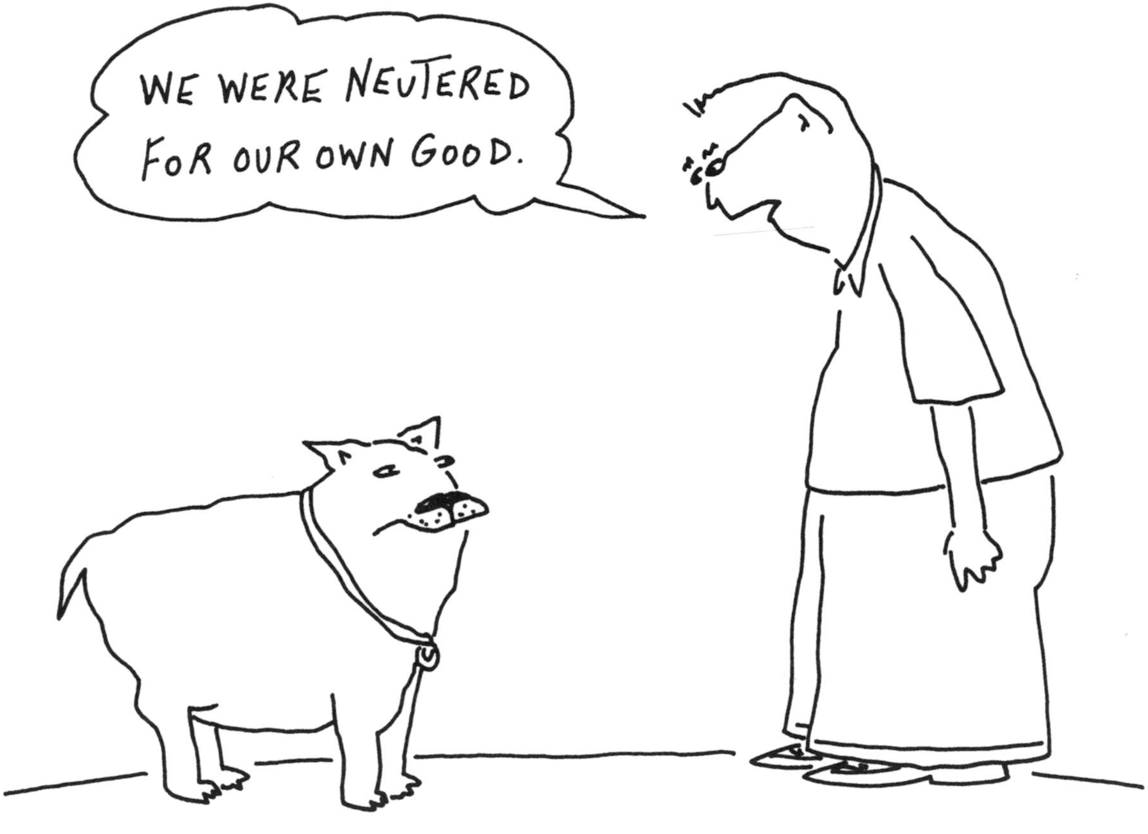
WE WERE NEUTERED FOR OUR OWN GOOD.

GOOD BOY

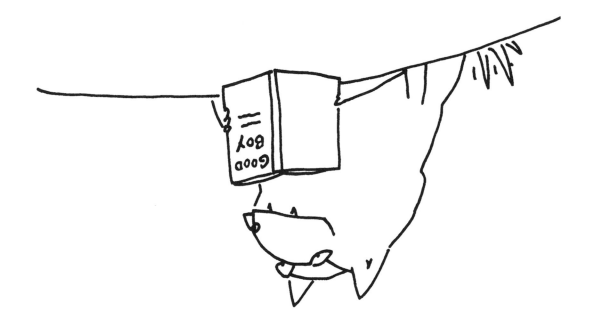

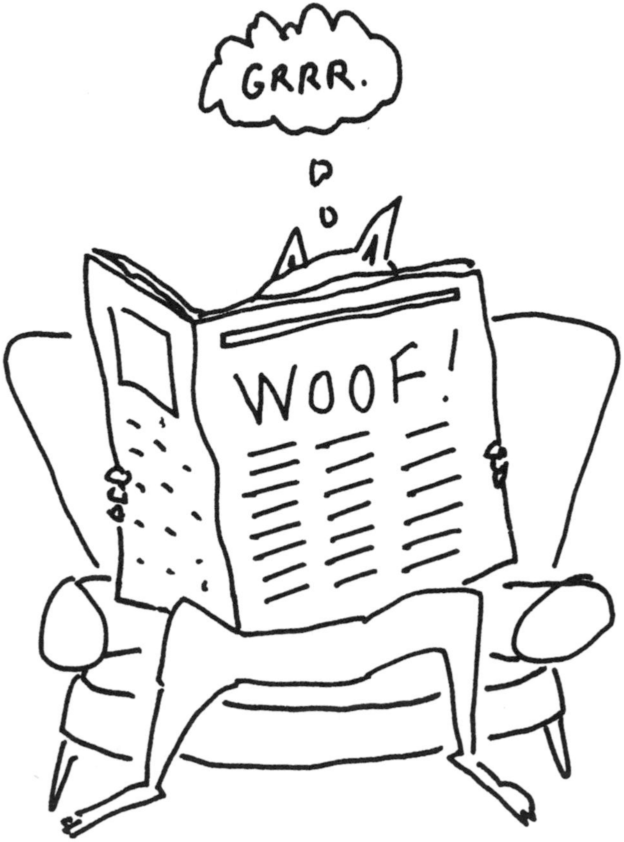
GRRR.
WOOF!

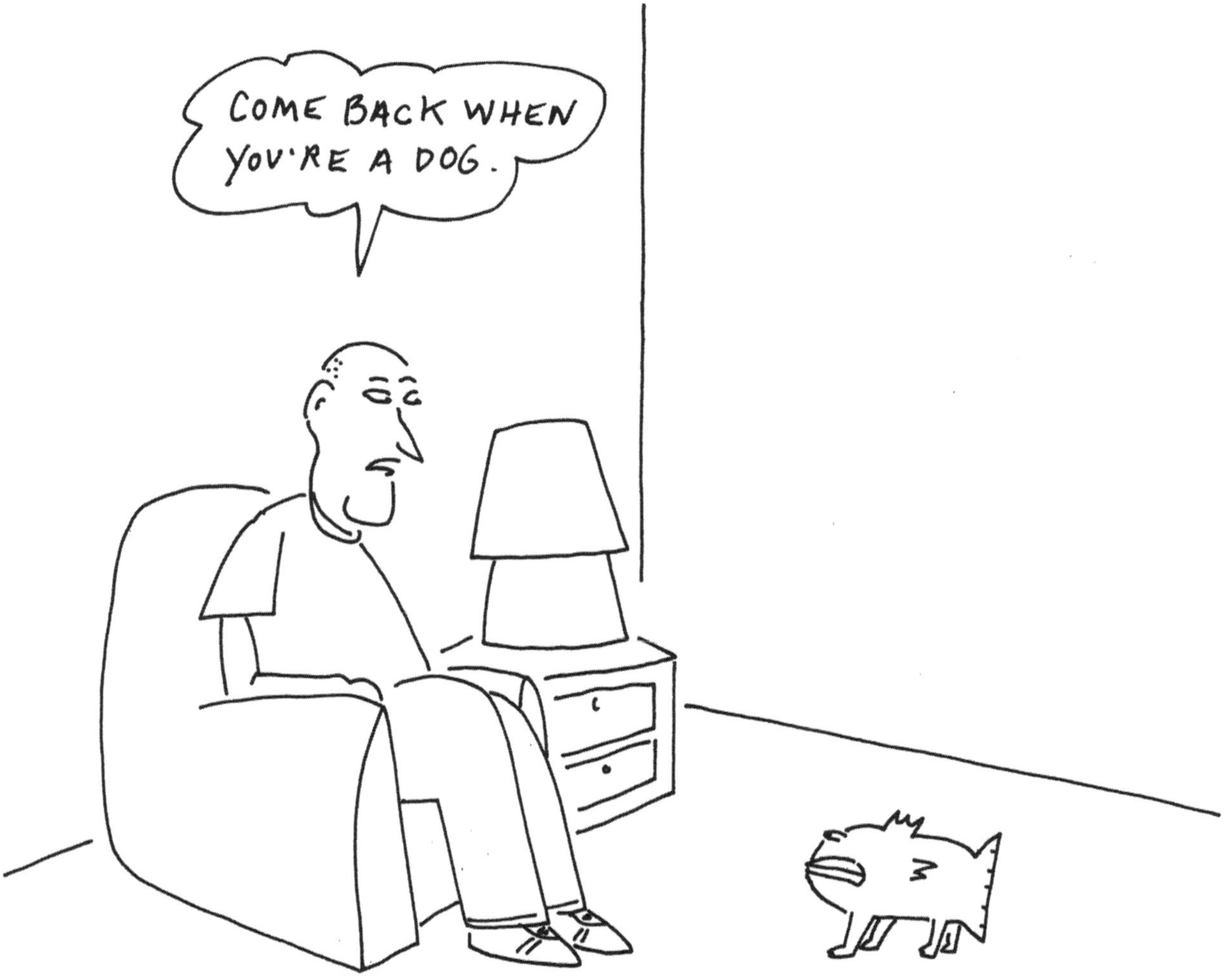
COME BACK WHEN YOU'RE A DOG.

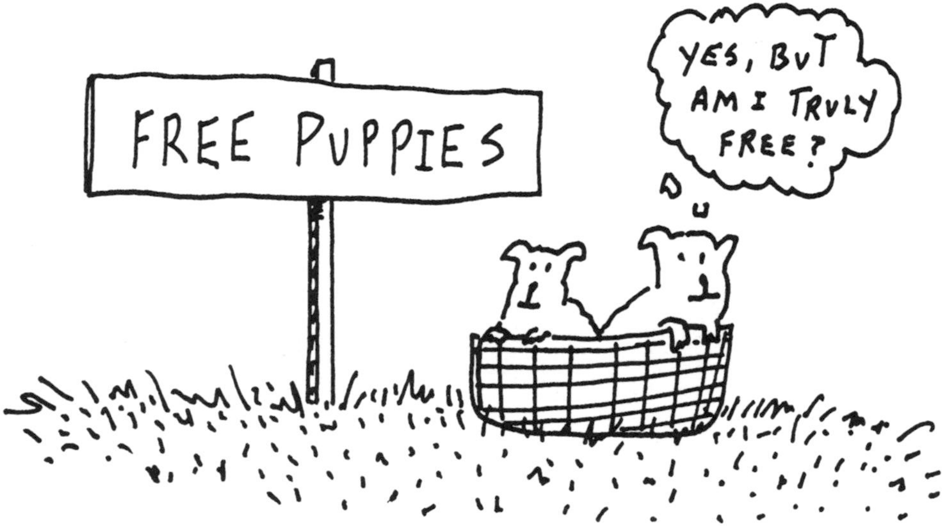
FREE PUPPIES
YES, BUT AM I TRULY FREE?

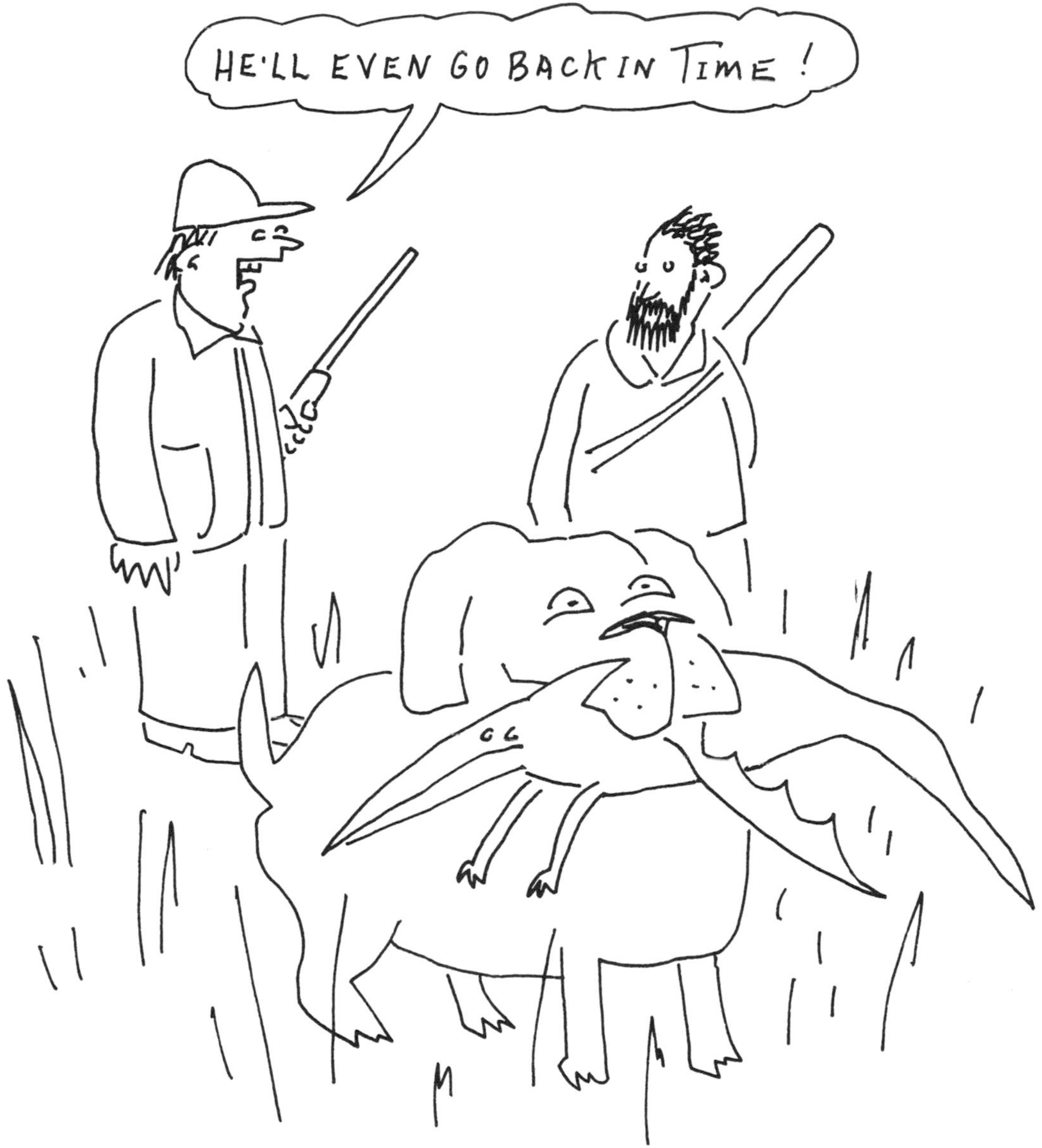
HE'LL EVEN GO BACK IN TIME!

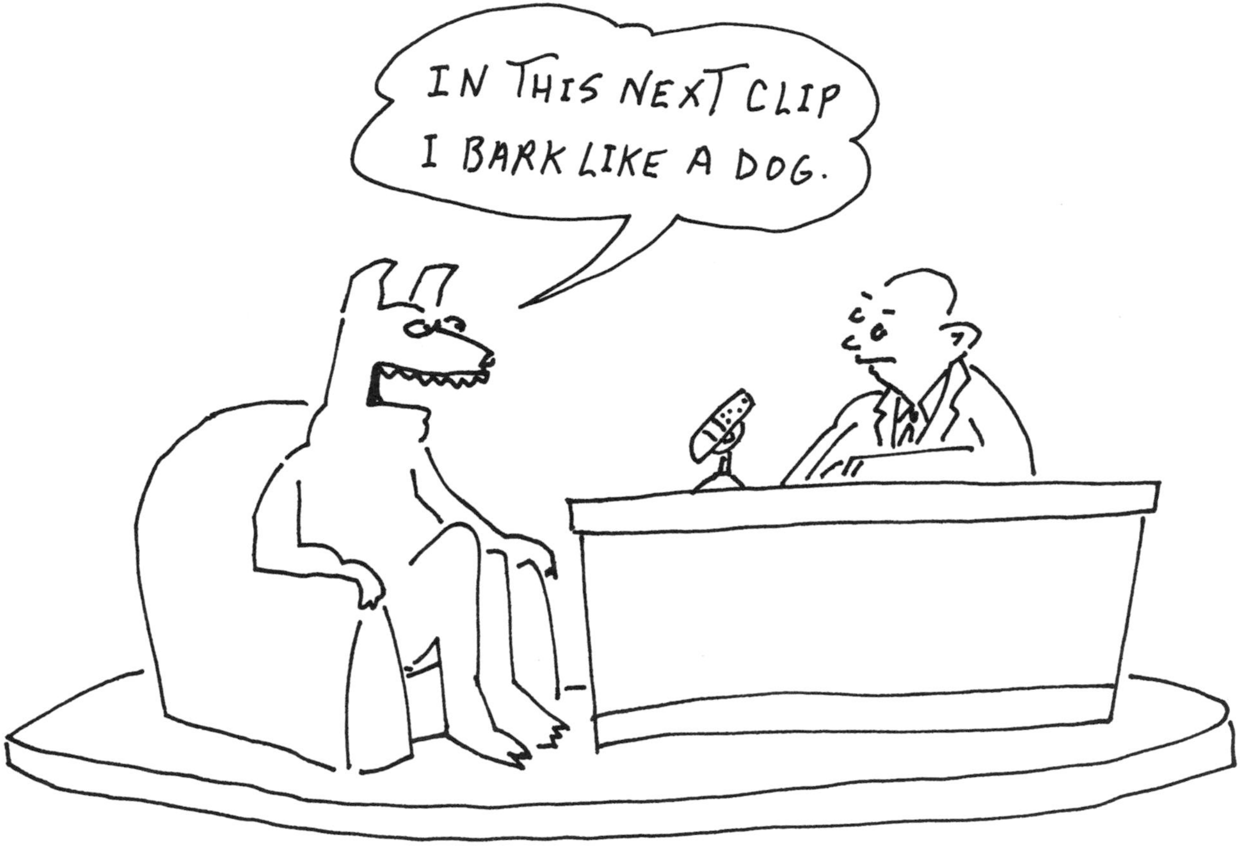
IN THIS NEXT CLIP I BARK LIKE A DOG.

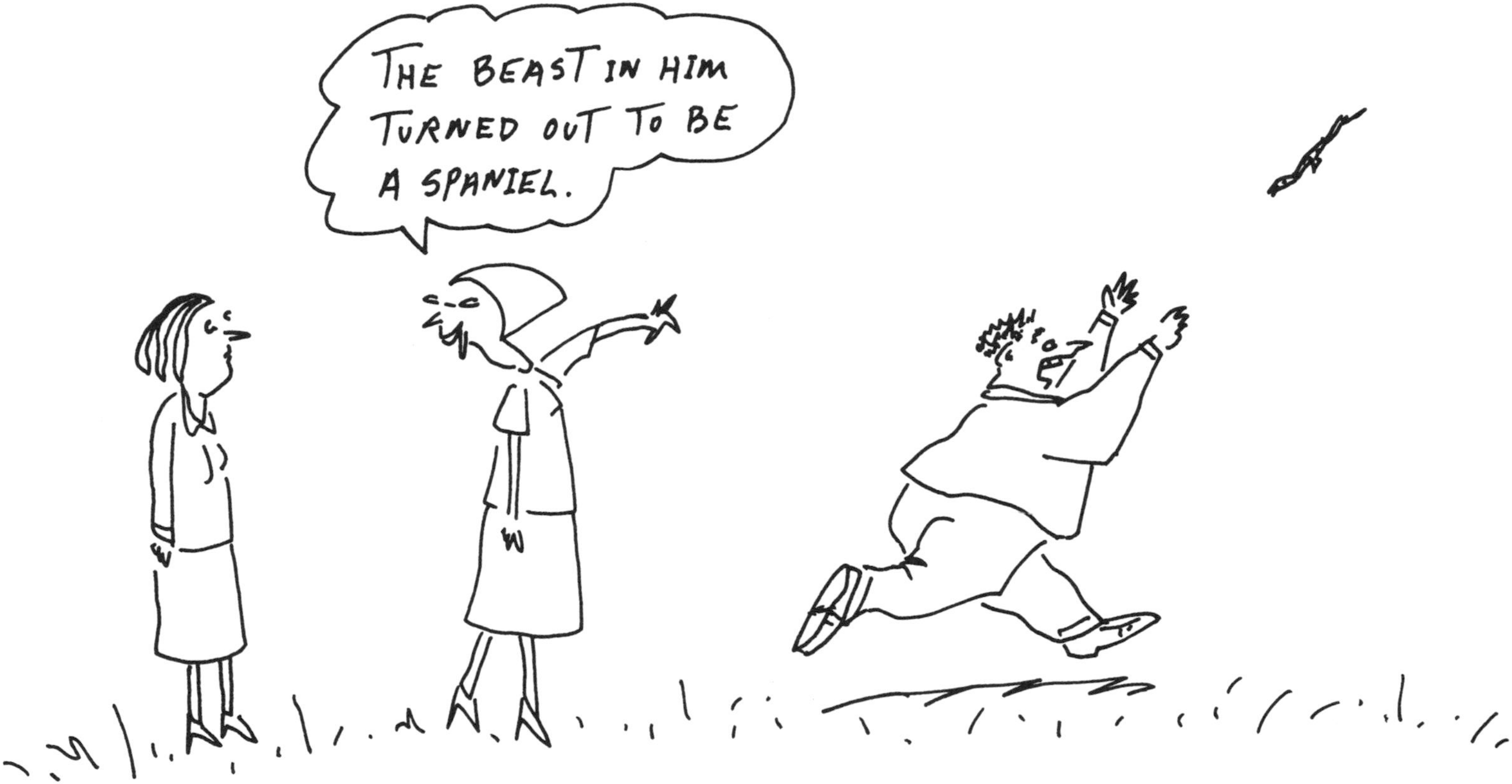
THE BEAST IN HIM TURNED OUT TO BE A SPANIEL.

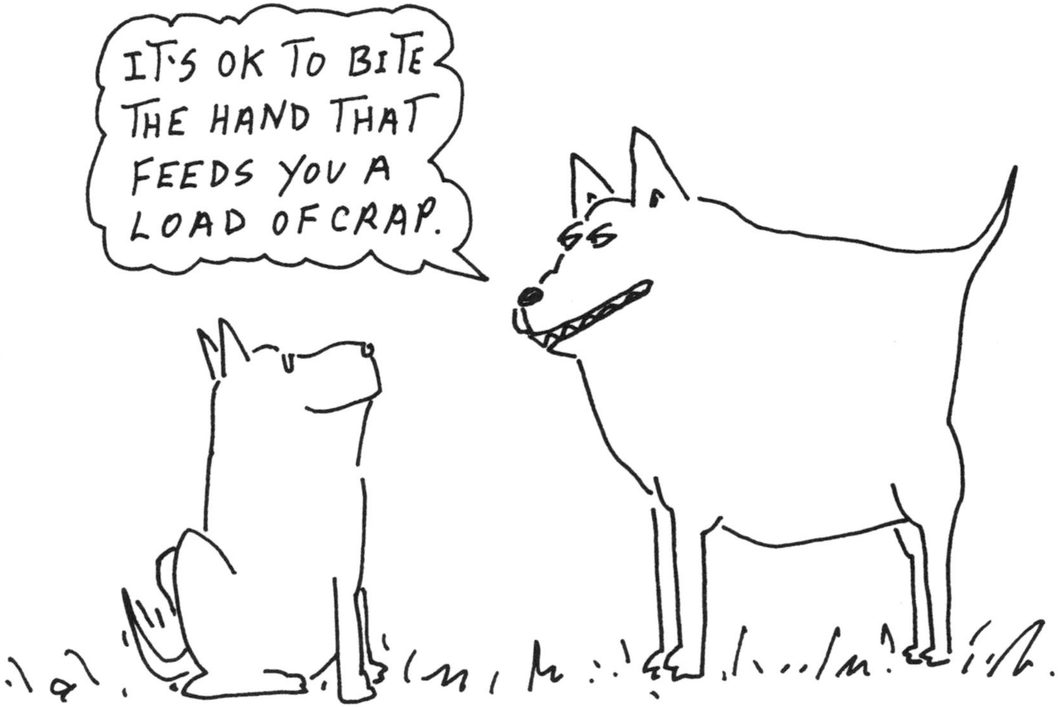
IT'S OK TO BITE THE HAND THAT FEEDS YOU A LOAD OF CRAP.

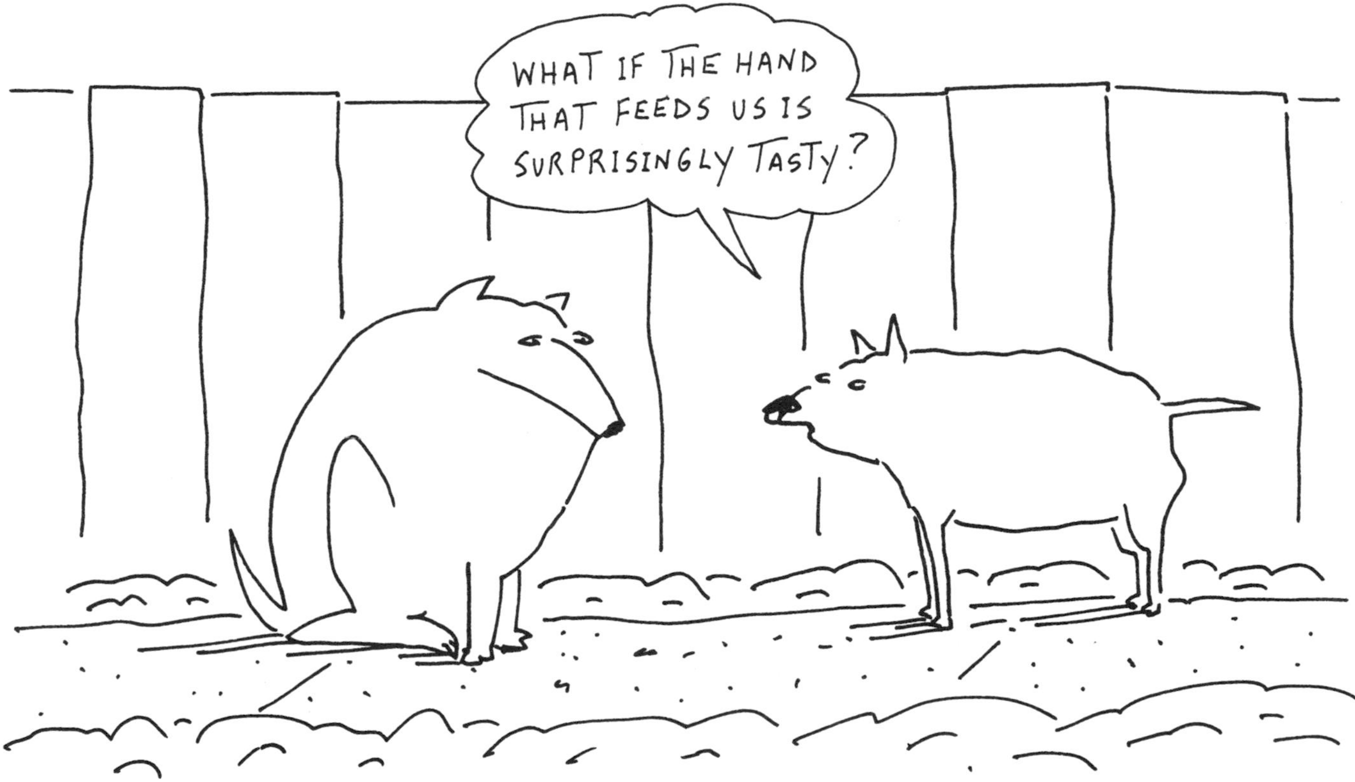
WHAT IF THE HAND THAT FEEDS US IS SURPRISINGLY TASTY?

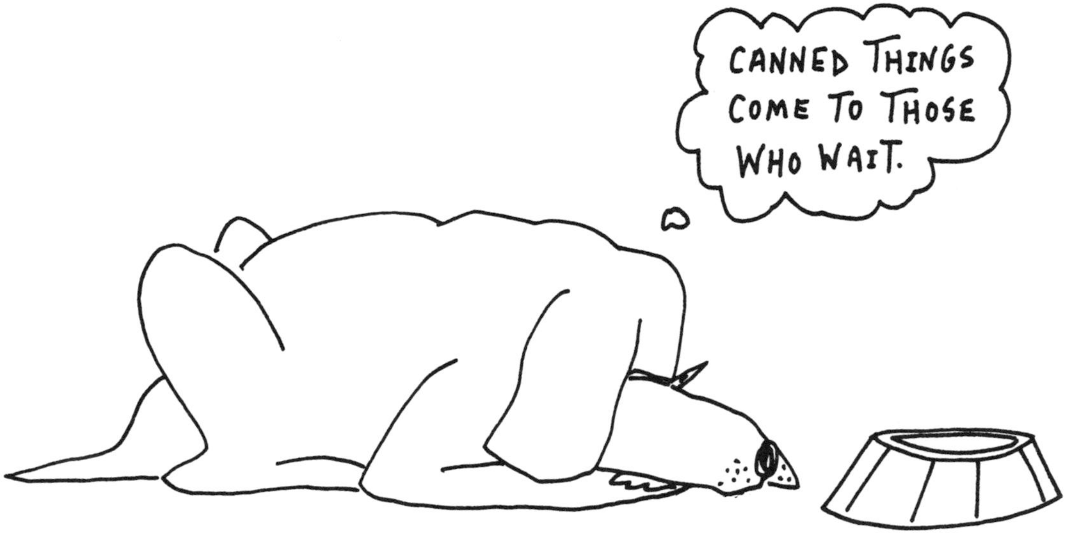
CANNED THINGS COME TO THOSE WHO WAIT.

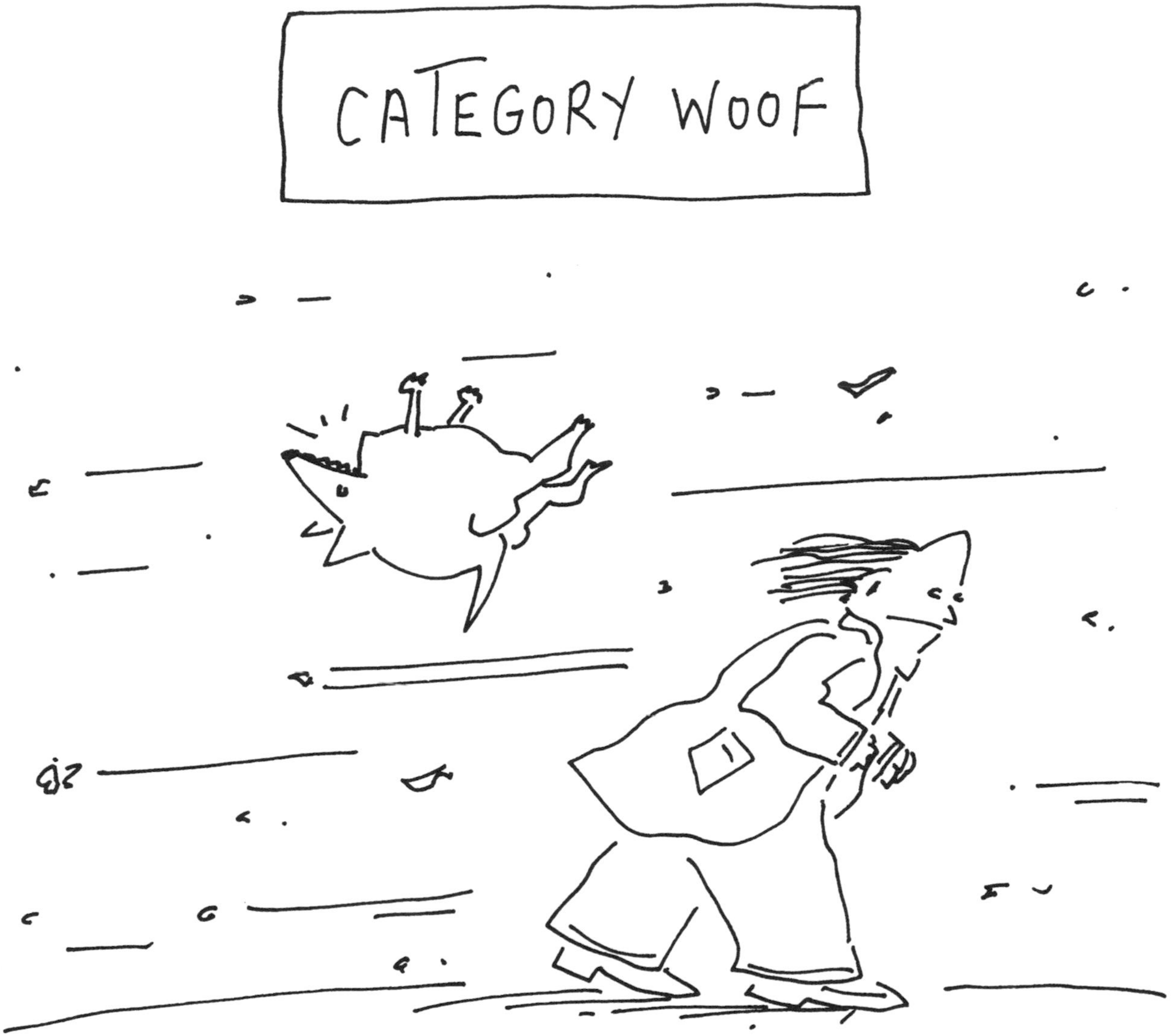
CATEGORY WOOF

SHAR·PEI FACELIFT

I'M LOSING MY DESIRE TO CHASE CARS.

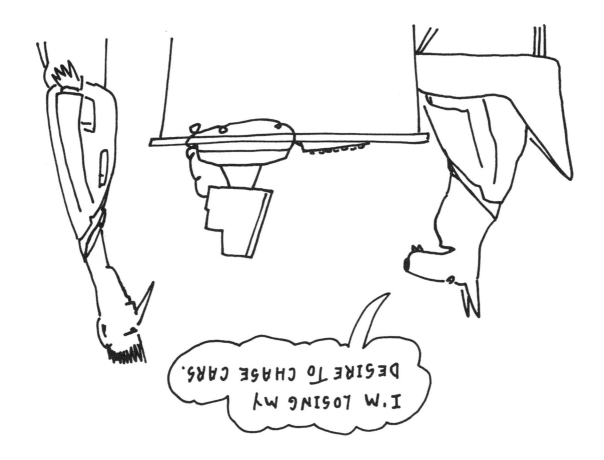

# THE DOG OF CONSEQUENCES

DON'T MAKE ME BARK OR I'LL BITE.

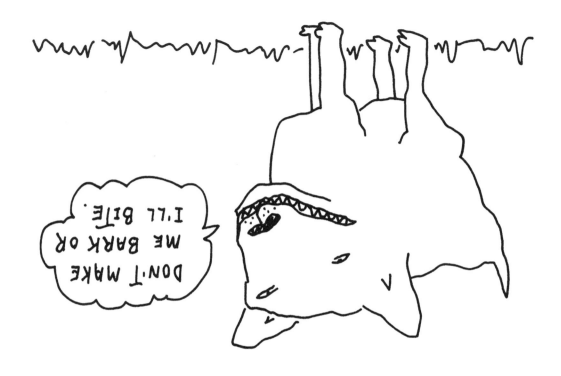

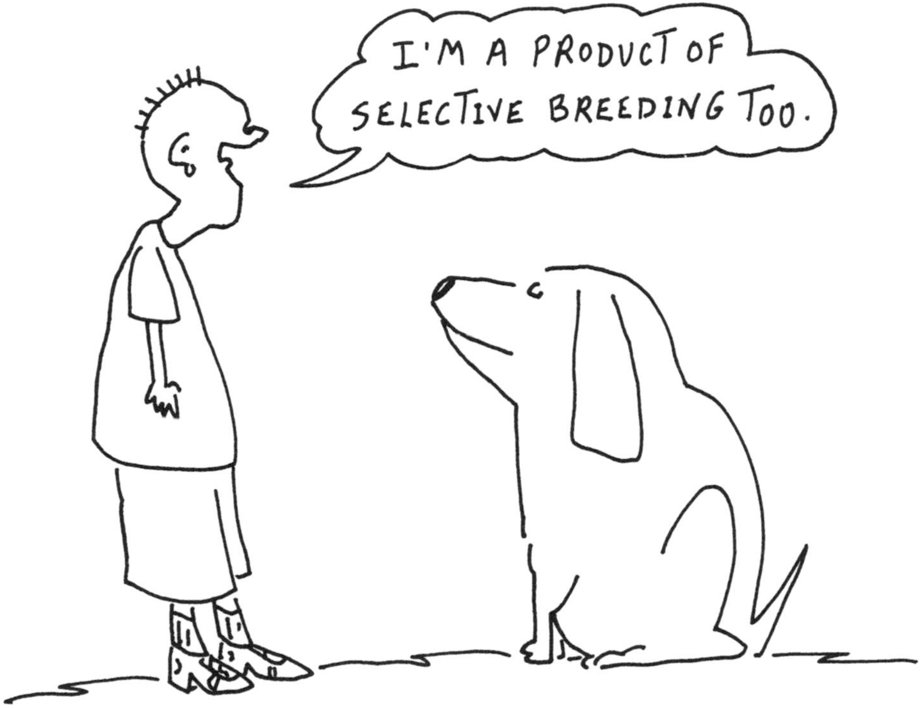
I'M A PRODUCT OF SELECTIVE BREEDING TOO.

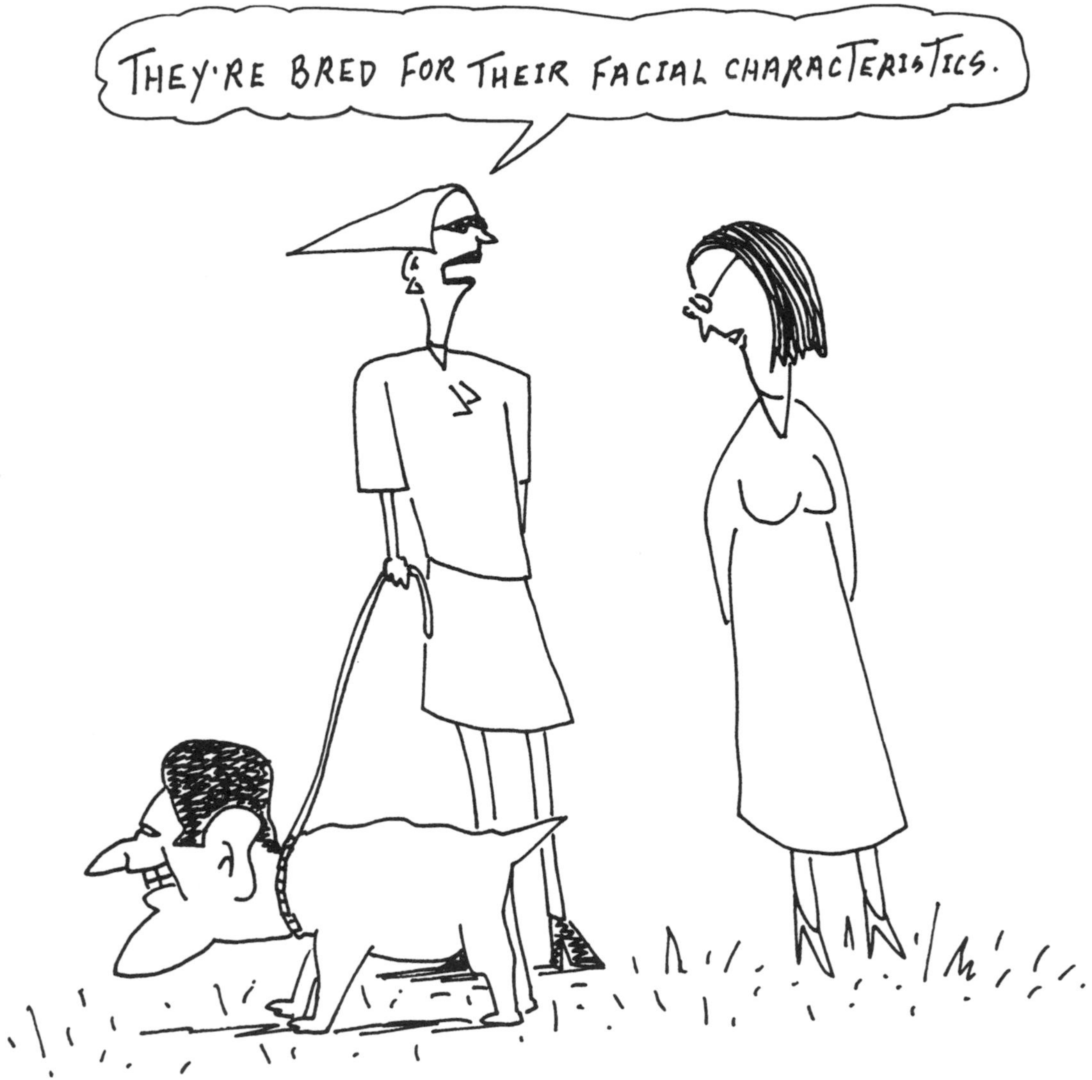
THEY'RE BRED FOR THEIR FACIAL CHARACTERISTICS.

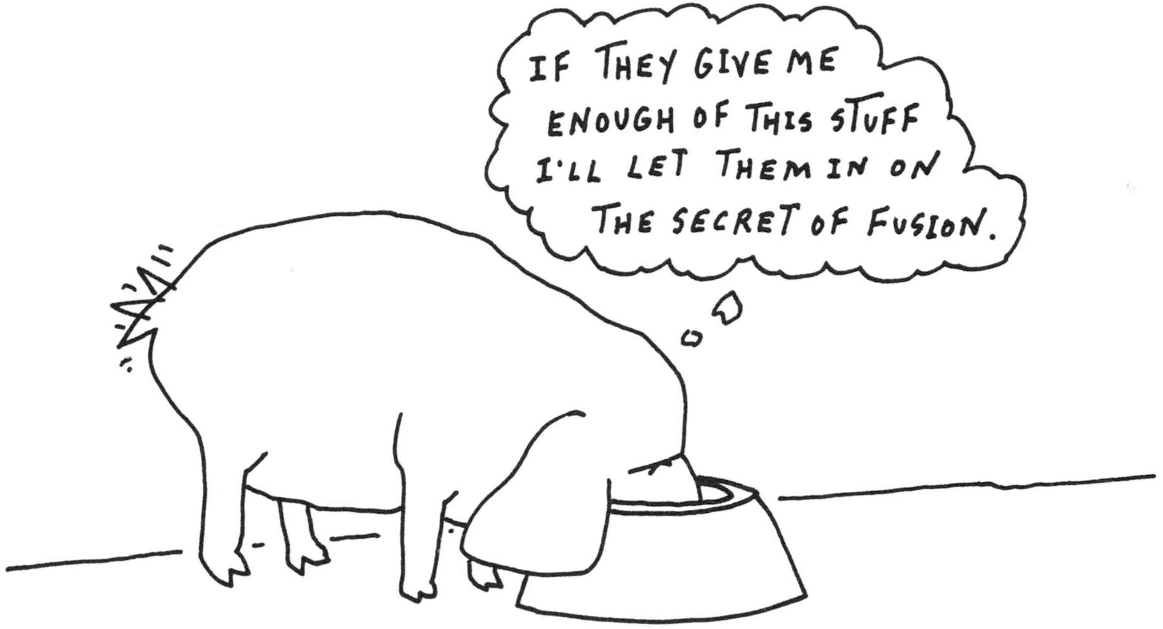
IF THEY GIVE ME ENOUGH OF THIS STUFF I'LL LET THEM IN ON THE SECRET OF FUSION.

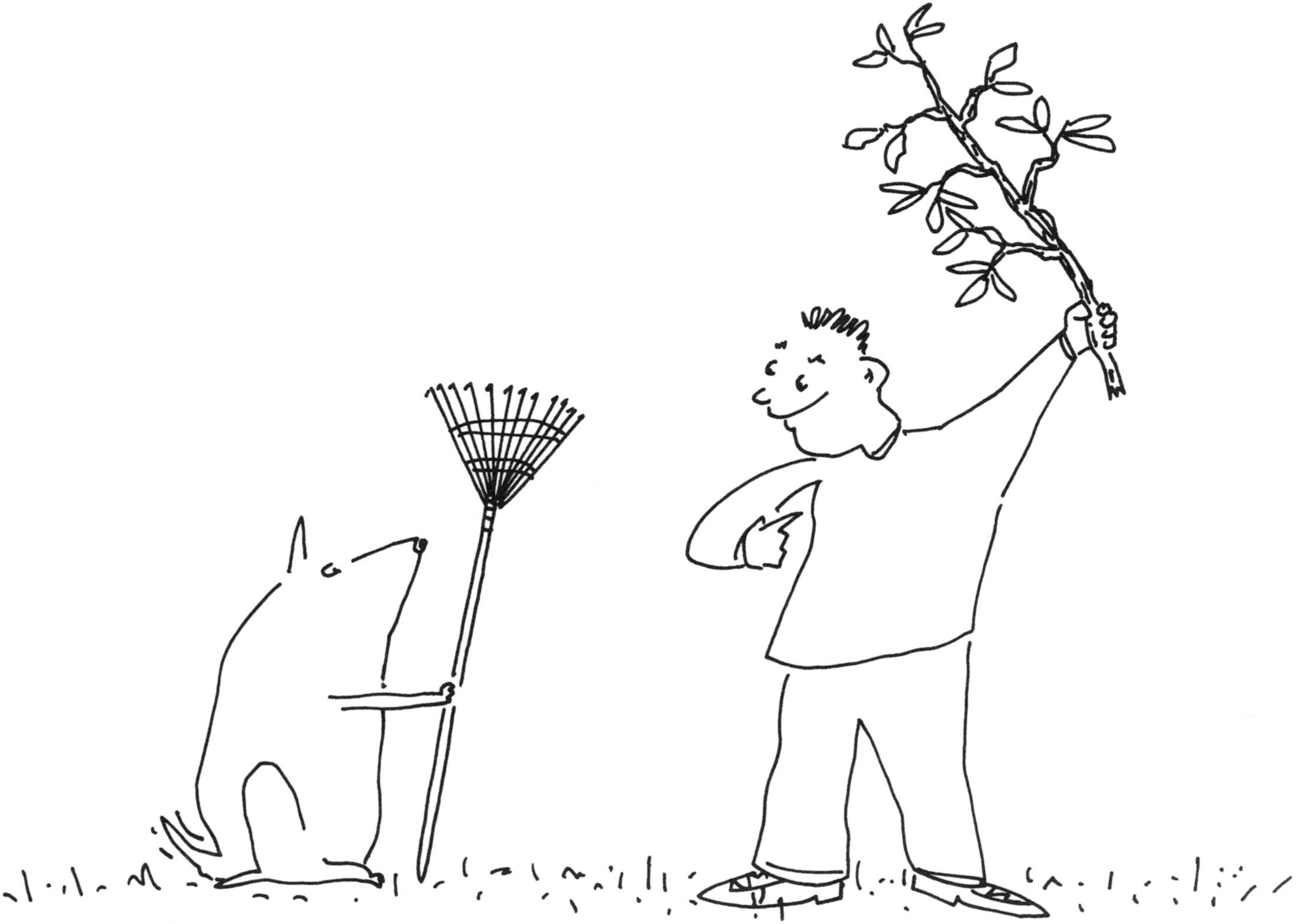

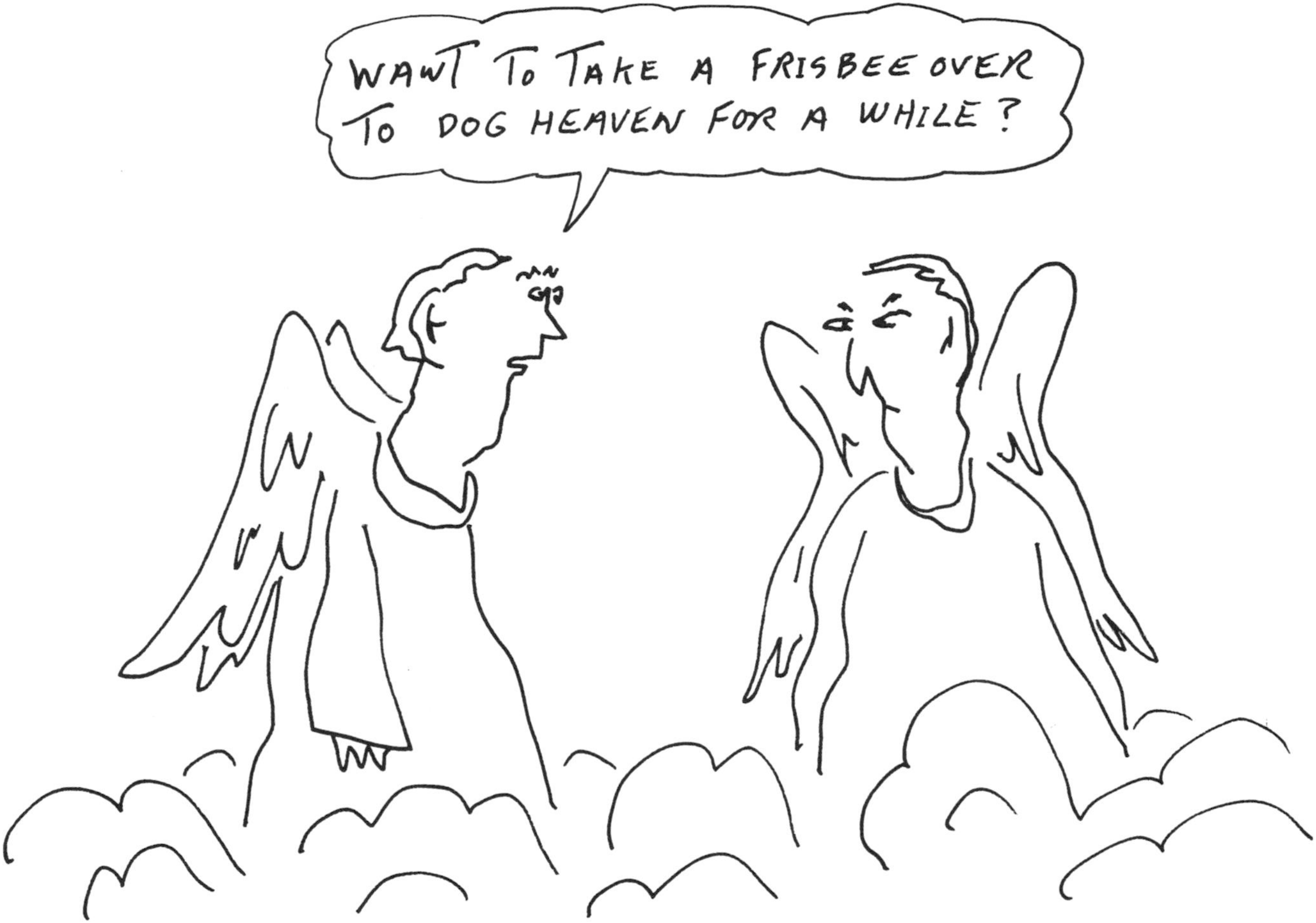
WANT TO TAKE A FRISBEE OVER TO DOG HEAVEN FOR A WHILE?

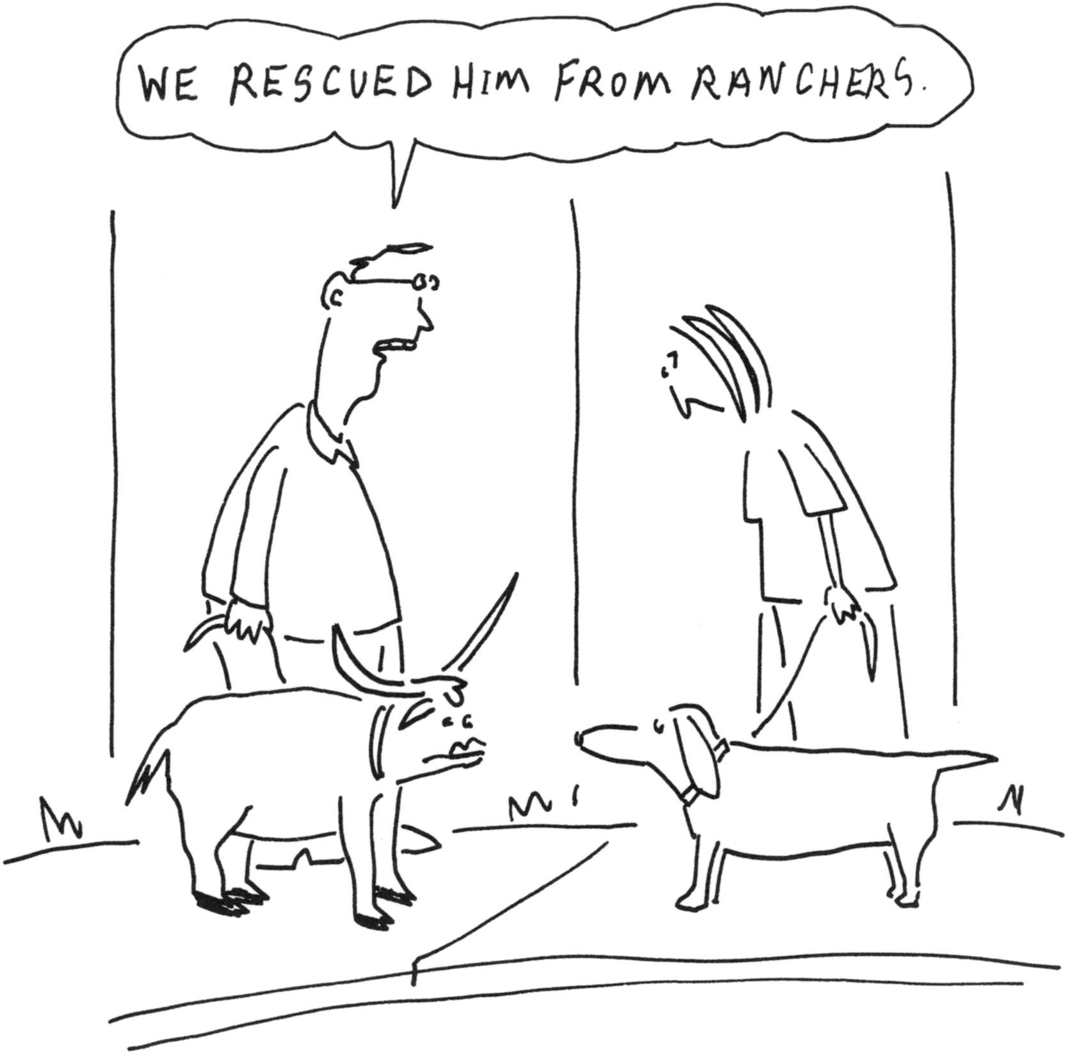
WE RESCUED HIM FROM RANCHERS.

THE HOUNDS OF HECK

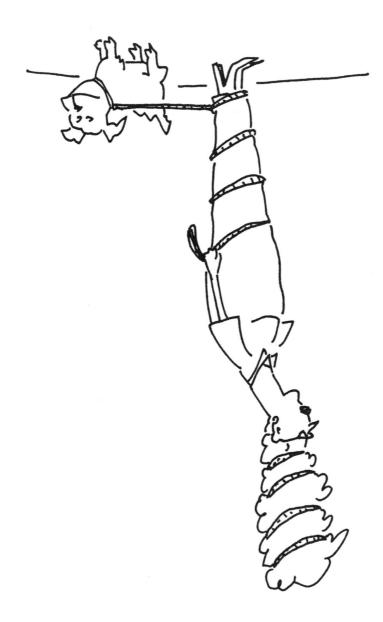

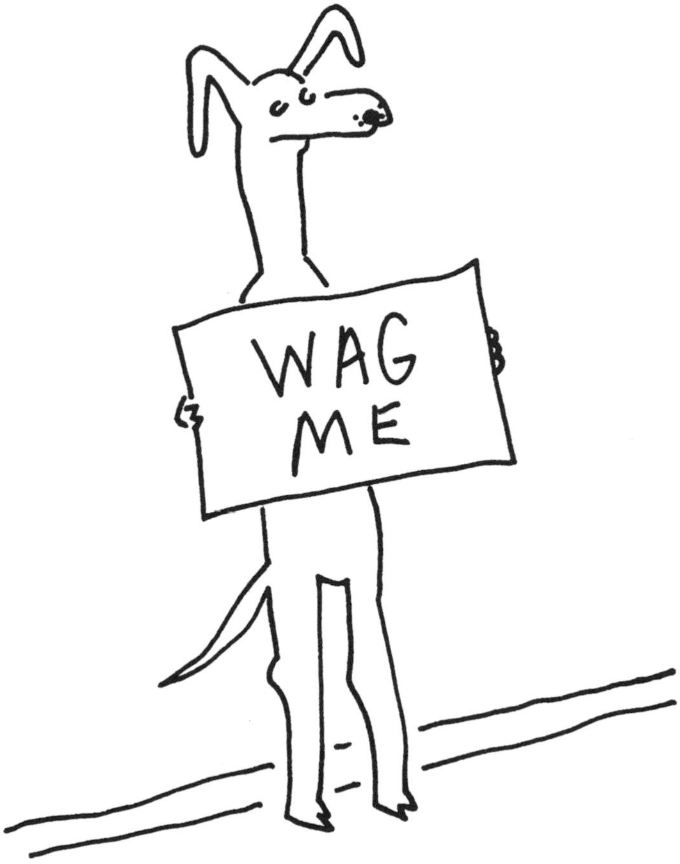
WAG
ME

LAPDOG

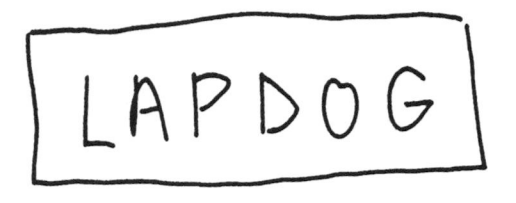

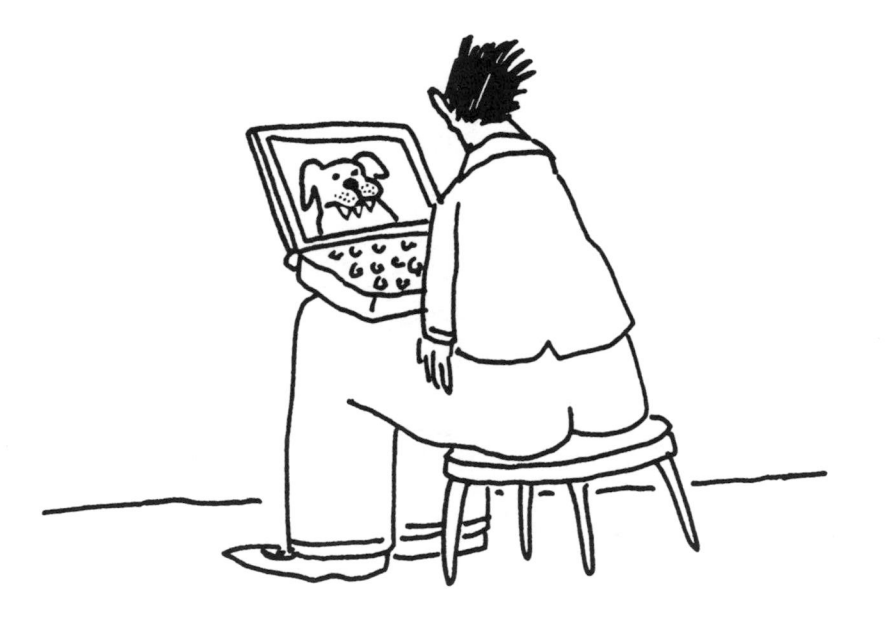

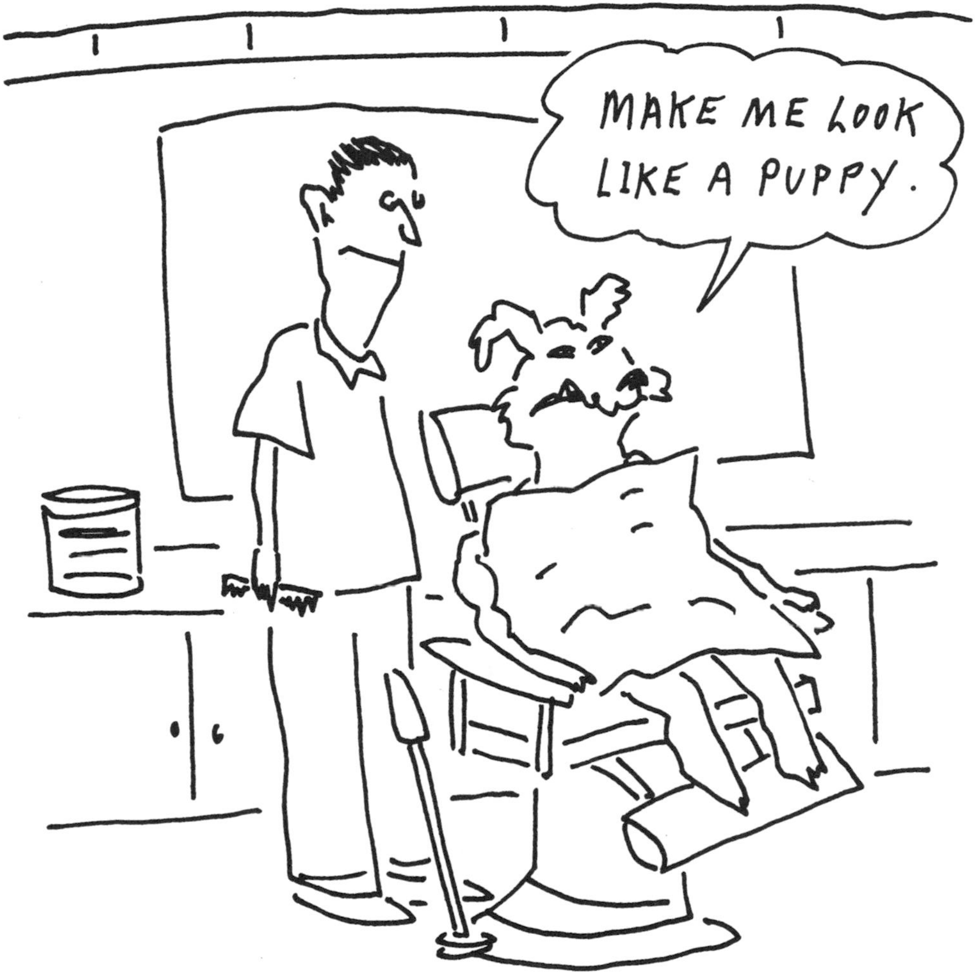
MAKE ME LOOK LIKE A PUPPY.

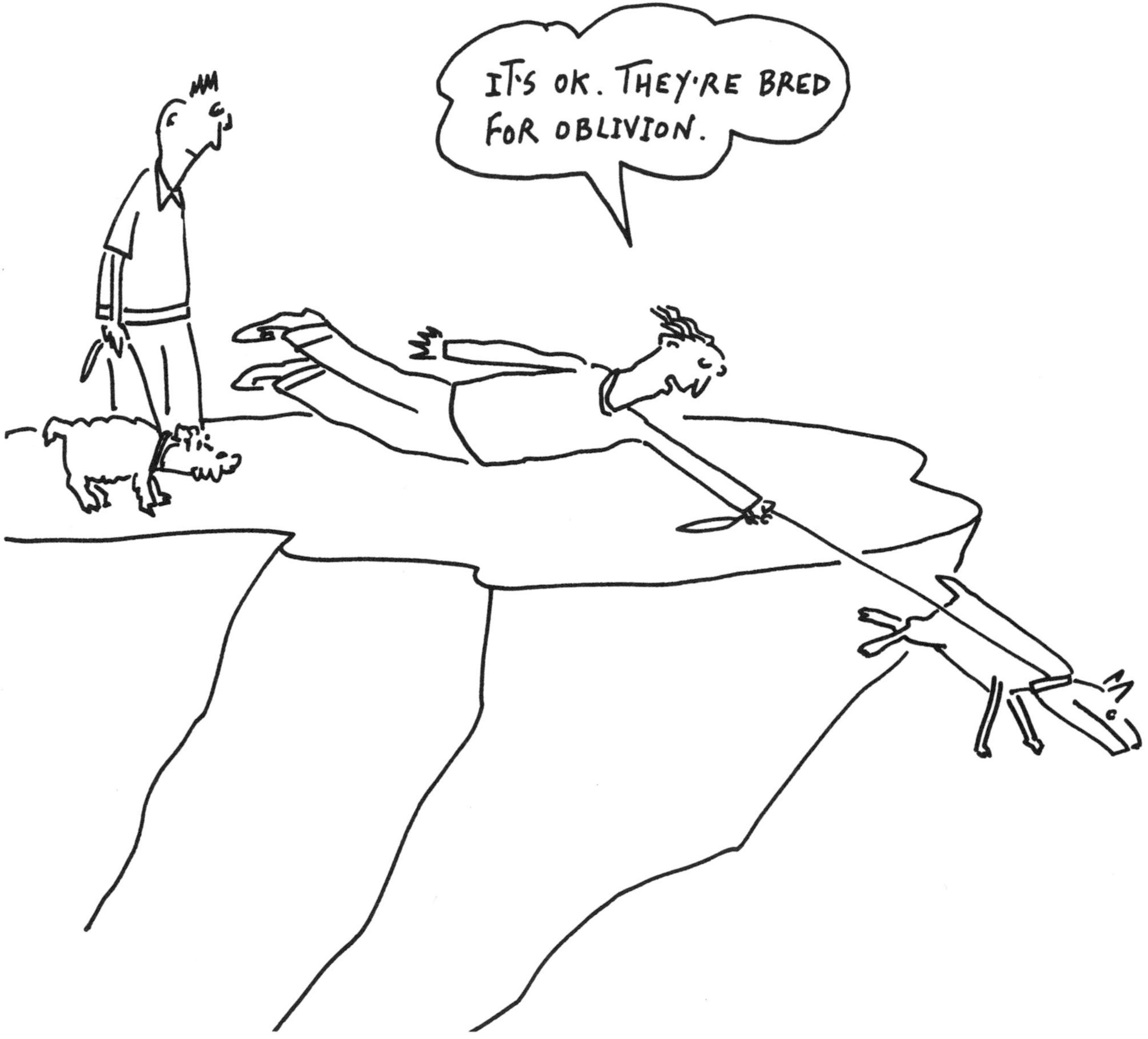
IT'S OK. THEY'RE BRED FOR OBLIVION.

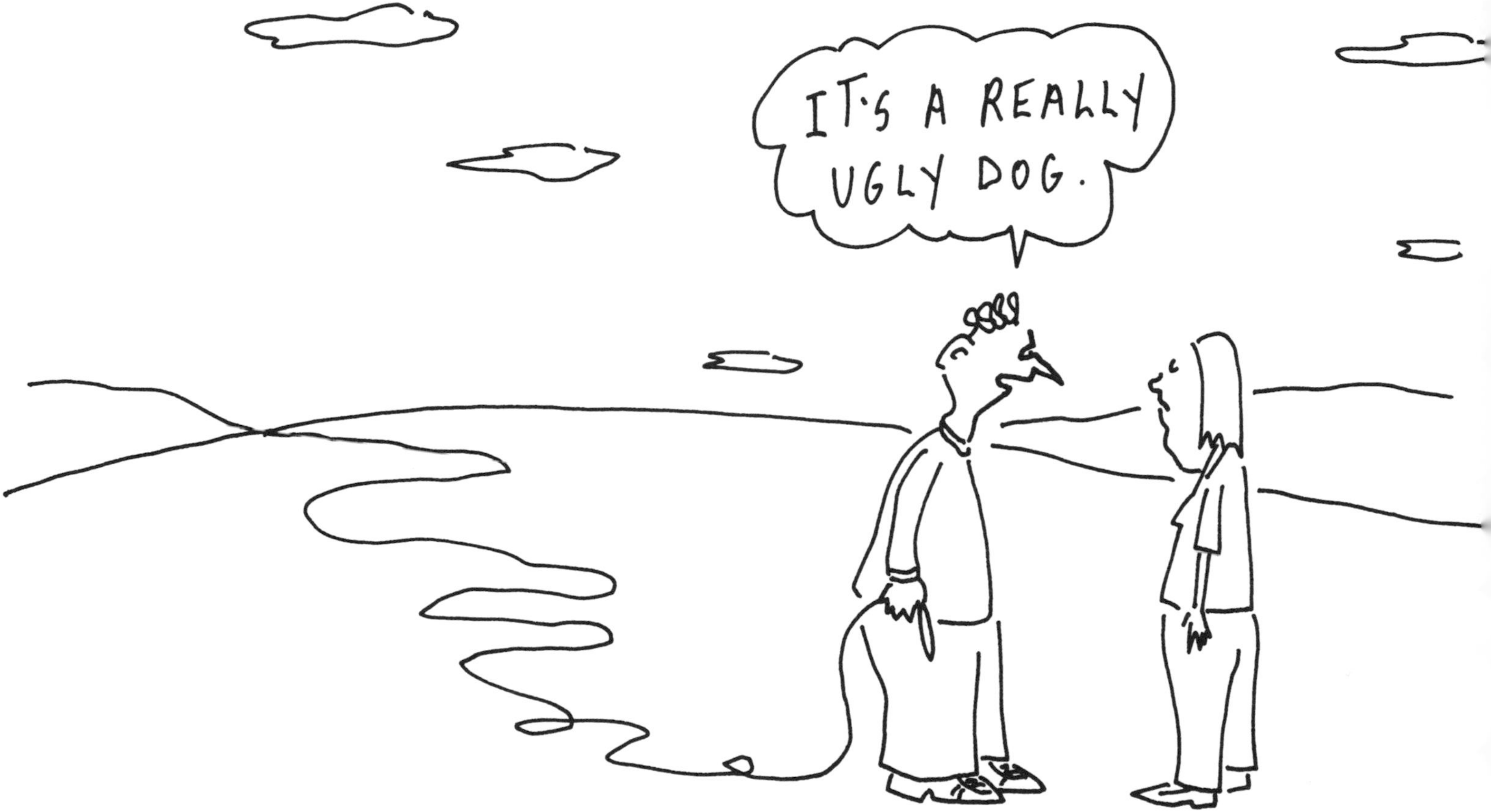
IT'S A REALLY UGLY DOG.

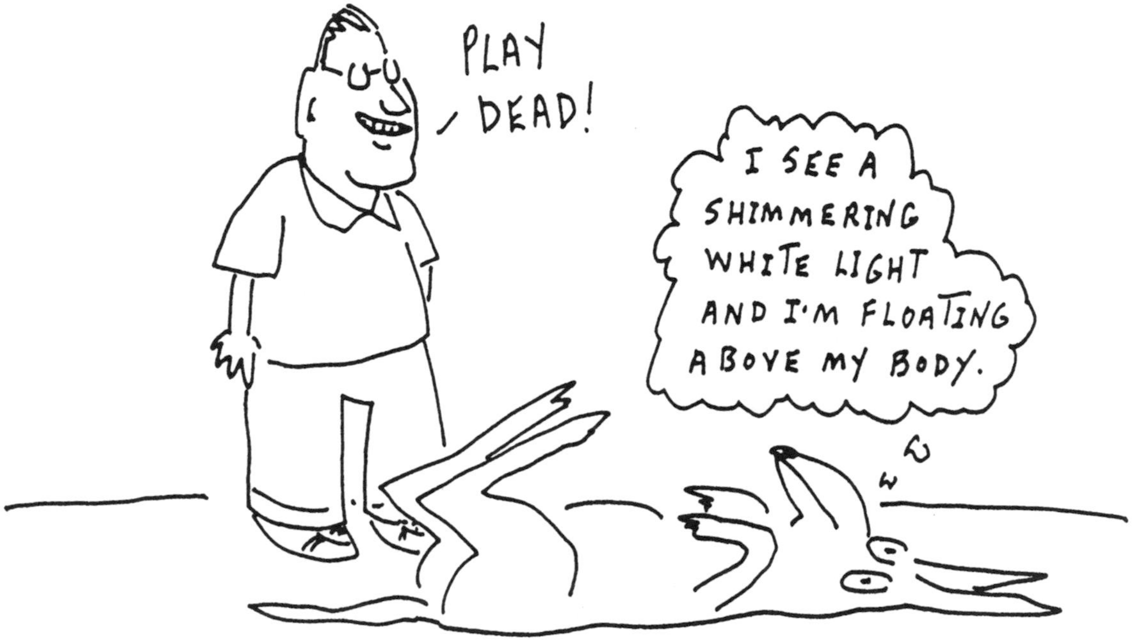
PLAY DEAD!
I SEE A SHIMMERING WHITE LIGHT AND I'M FLOATING ABOVE MY BODY.

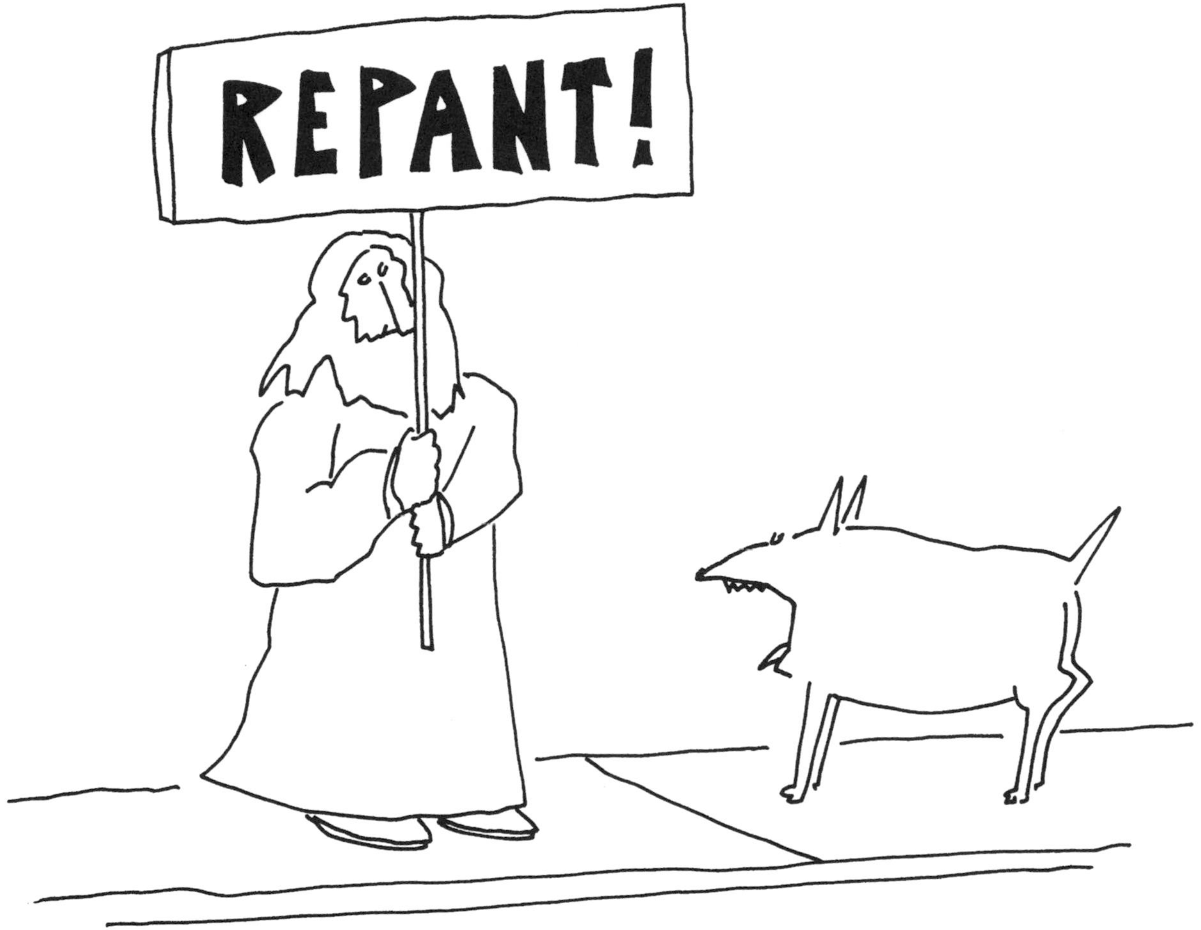
REPANT!

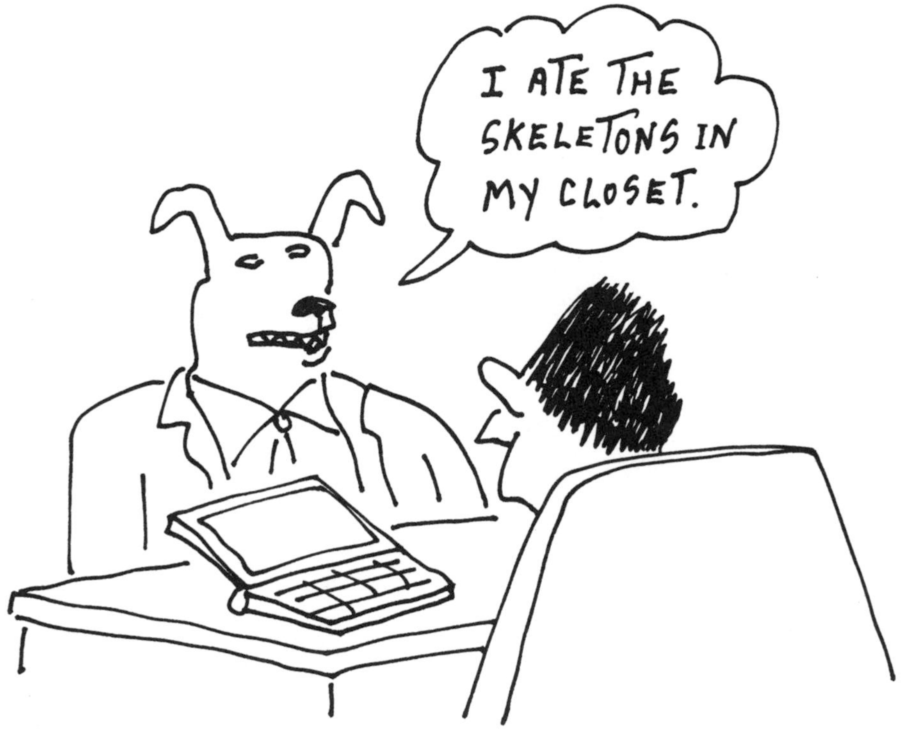
I ATE THE SKELETONS IN MY CLOSET.

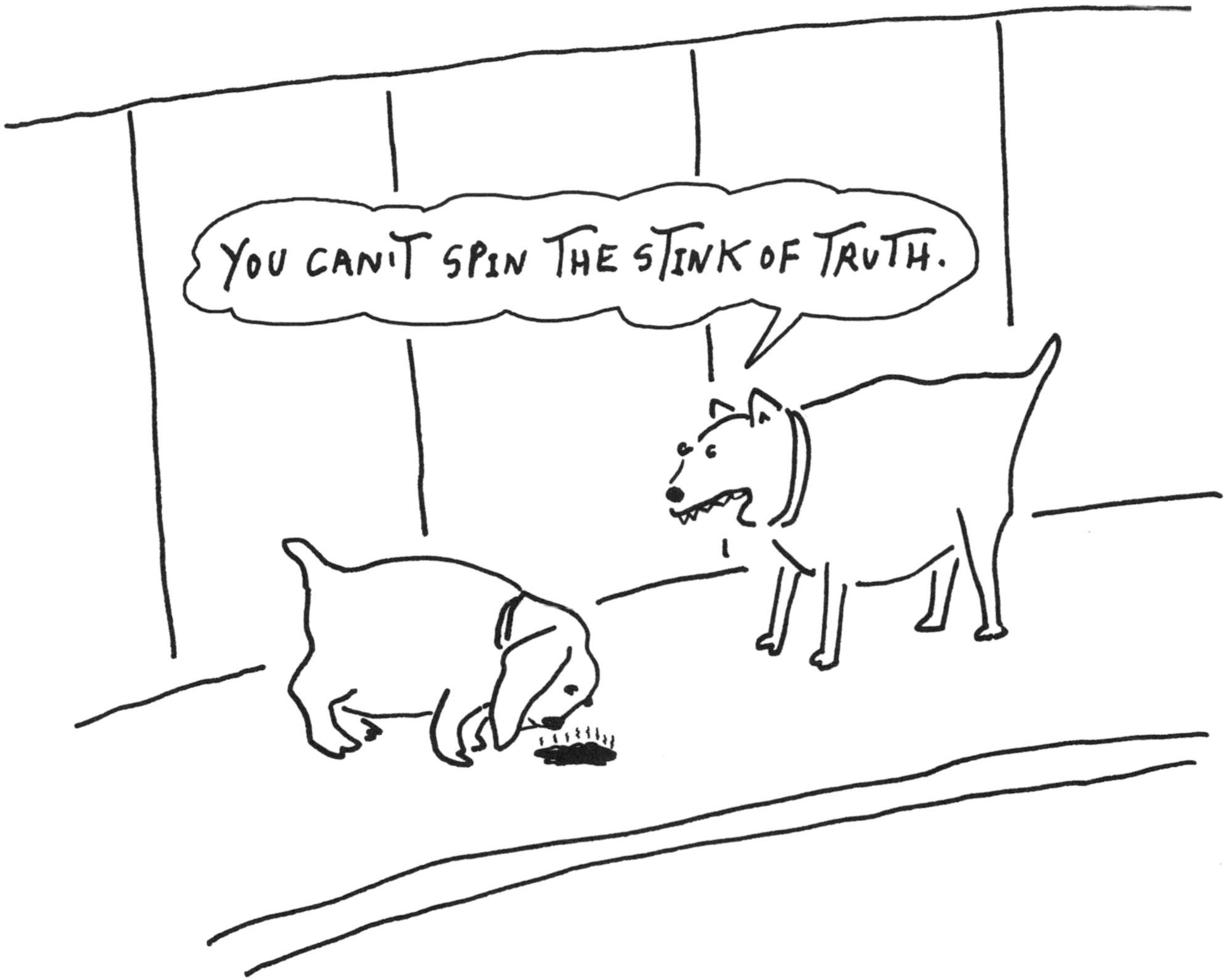
YOU CAN'T SPIN THE STINK OF TRUTH.

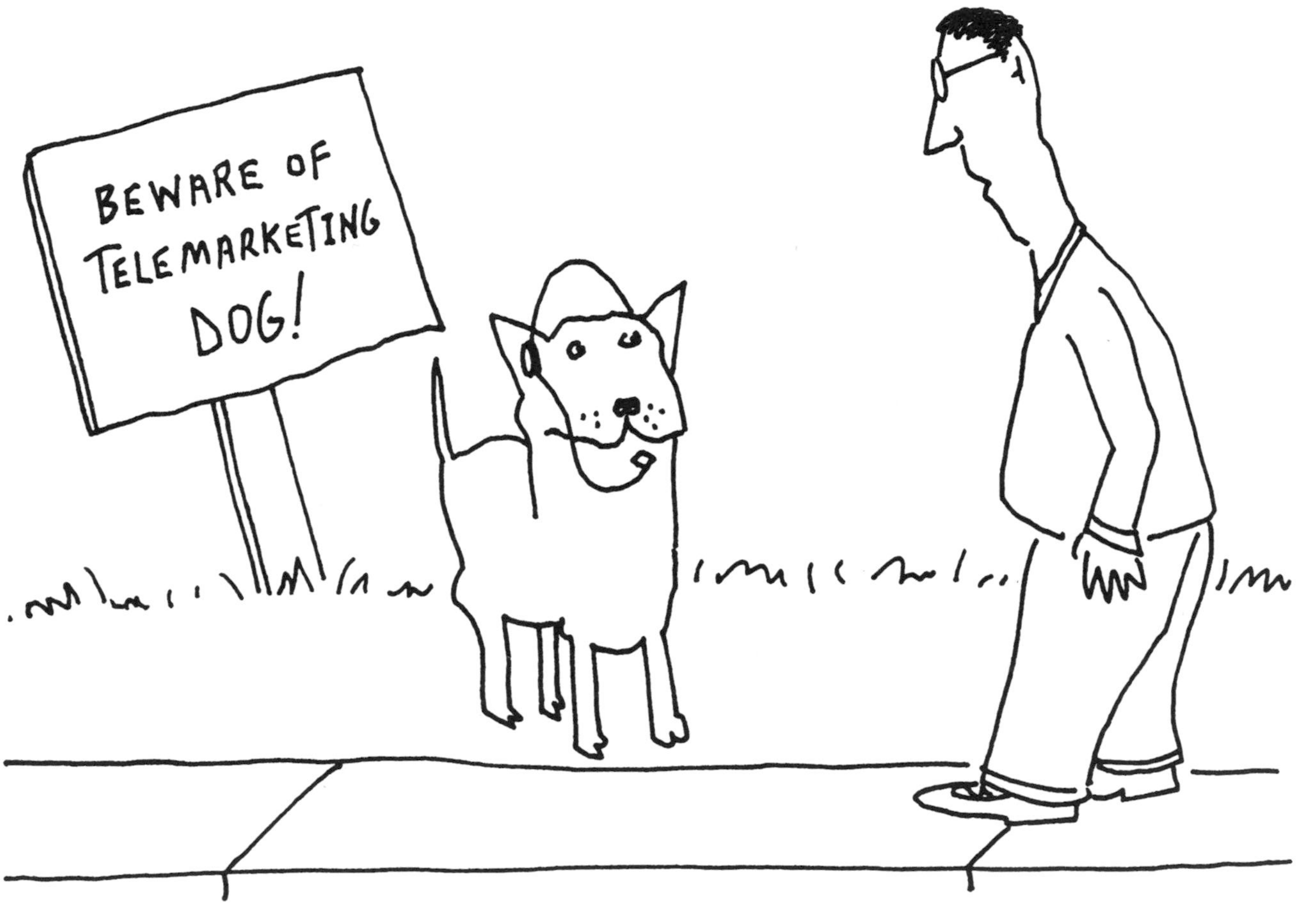
BEWARE OF
TELEMARKETING
DOG!

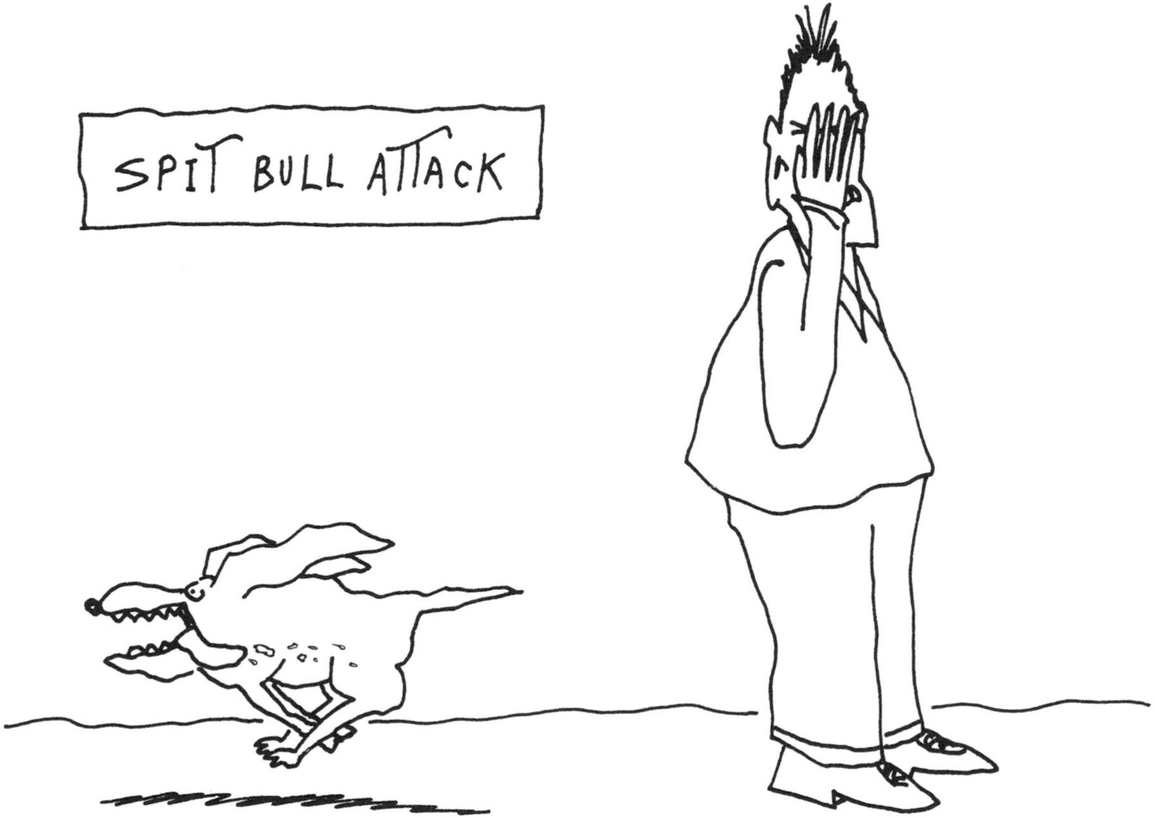
SPIT BULL ATTACK

I'M A TALKING DOG. ARE YOU PREPARED TO LISTEN?

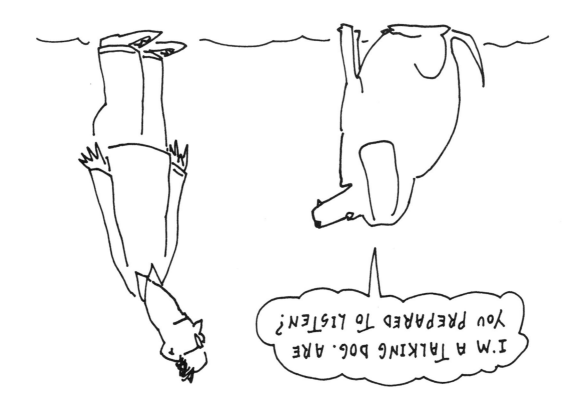

WORK LIKE A DOG.
PLAY LIKE A DOG.

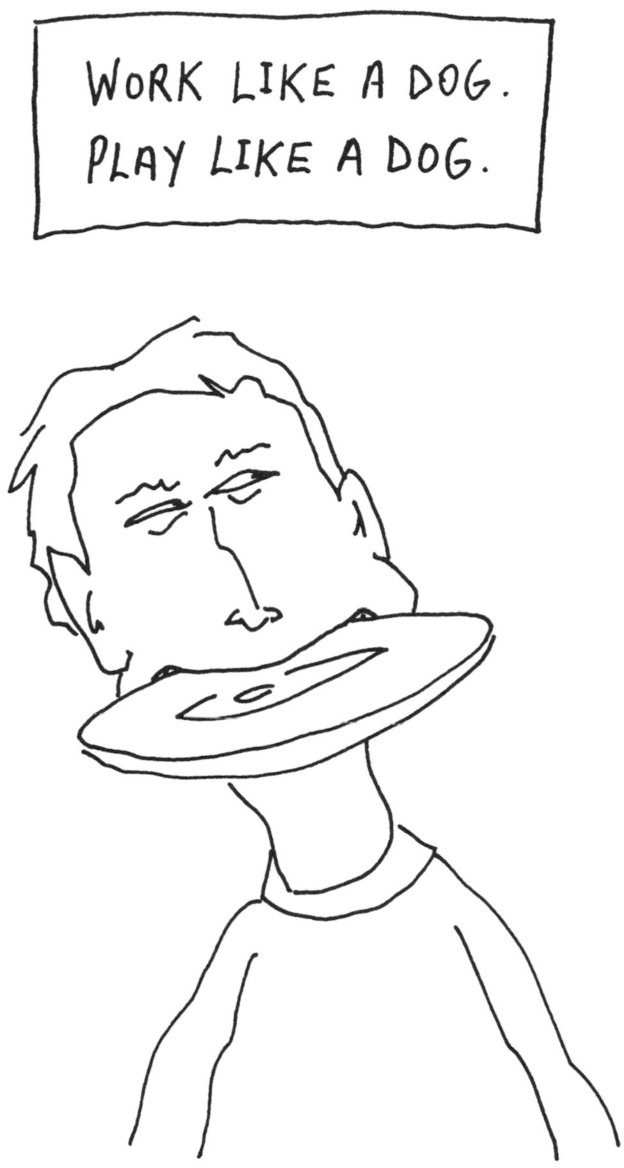